Six Functions, One Vision

SIX FUNCTIONS ONE VISION

A PRACTICAL GUIDE
— for —
MODERN LEADERS

DOROTHY KUDLA

LIONCREST
PUBLISHING

SIX FUNCTIONS, ONE VISION
A Practical Guide for Modern Leaders

FIRST EDITION

ISBN   978-1-5445-4696-4 *Hardcover*
           978-1-5445-4695-7 *Paperback*
           978-1-5445-4697-1 *Ebook*

To those who believed in me, encouraged me, and weren't afraid to call me out—I'm forever grateful.

And to every person who steps into leadership and makes a difference, this book is for you. You make this world a better place.

CONTENTS

FOREWORD

—DAVID WALMSLEY, EDITOR IN CHIEF, *THE GLOBE AND MAIL*

Quick. Think. Who is the greatest leader you have worked with? Then pause. As you let the kettle boil reflecting on the question, several sensations appear. Your first answer probably isn't the final answer. Your final answer probably surprises you, and in between you have ranked a full range of personalities you have met in different circumstances.

What you are experiencing is the sense that leadership must move with the times.

Which brings me to this book and the author Dorothy Kudla. I first met Dorothy more than a decade ago when *The Globe and Mail* invited her in. The news organization was keen to develop existing and upcoming managers and provide the training that could make them leaders.

As you can imagine, news organizations are complex, with a range of humanity on display every day internally and in the news.

Within a newsroom, seniority is less respected than competence. Integrity is an absolute, but perennial commercial disruption tries to corrode the already neurotic confidence of daily whim that is organized news.

Layered over that is a desire, indeed a duty, to make sense of an inchoate world, often involving a seemingly endless set of perilous uncontrollable events.

Into this melting pot came Dorothy. And we didn't make it easy for her, especially those staff in the newsroom who were born to be skeptics and determined to disrupt. Me included.

"The work never stops," "the pressures are so acute," "nobody seems to understand what I have to do." That's how the first sessions were taken up. A list of victimhood complaints. Not our finest hour, but the airing of them was essential to move toward the honesty of ideas that were to be exchanged in the years to come.

With aplomb, driven as much by a superb listening ear as by the skills taught, Dorothy won us over. She listened to the challenges and the skepticism and teased the silent ones to speak out. It began to dawn on everyone that nobody has the answers immediately, but they emerge through consideration and empathy.

This book isn't bafflegab and the teachings aren't ethereal. Dorothy is the most practical teacher imaginable. She had to be for the newsroom to accept her. Dorothy's relationship with *The Globe and Mail* is among her longest partnerships, and she has been invited back year after year because she helps both emerging leaders in the company and senior leadership. Me included.

Even today, when we face personnel challenges, those who have been provided training will often say out loud in a meeting: "What would Dorothy do?" In some ways, it is the ultimate compliment.

And that's why I find myself in the unusual geography of writing this foreword.

As you will find in reading *Six Functions, One Vision: A Practical Guide for Modern Leaders*, the competing experiences of your daily job, regardless of where you work or how you work, are commonplace. They are also surmountable.

INTRODUCTION

It's possible that you've never caught even a few minutes of one of the dozens of superhero movies that have taken over entertainment culture in recent years, but I doubt it. Each hero is different, with a buildout of unique traits and abilities. But, if you look beyond the dazzling special effects and thrilling plots, they all have something in common:

The origin story.

No hero was born fully formed, ready to save the world—even the ones who started with some powers. It took an inciting event to set them on their journey, followed by self-discovery, learning, honing their skills, and growing.

This narrative isn't just confined to the screen; it parallels the making of a leader.

FINDING YOUR SUPERPOWER

Just like superheroes, leaders do not arrive in this world complete and fully formed. They must learn to harness their abilities and develop their skills intentionally and with purpose.

If you are reading this book, odds are you have something in common with that superhero. Maybe you have some inkling of your "superpower" but no clear road map for how to use it. Maybe you've been gifted with some theoretical leadership knowledge but haven't had the hands-on practice. Or maybe you killed it in a technical role, caught the attention of your higher-ups, and now you find yourself with a job title that didn't come with a blueprint for success. And if you've been at it for a while, your once-reliable superpower may not seem as strong as it used to.

Unfortunately, these scenarios are all too common. We're expected to lead with the expertise of a seasoned pro, yet we often lack the comprehensive understanding of how to do so. But we're still expected to get to where we need to be. Fast.

Imagine a superhero plucked from the front lines of fighting bad guys and planted in a new role where they were tasked with overseeing and maximizing the performance of heroes around the world. This shift—moving from excelling in a specific role to guiding and managing others—requires a completely different set of skills. How does a sales expert maximize the performance of a team with diverse skills and backgrounds? Or how does a software engineer, once focused on coding and problem-solving, suddenly manage a team with different technical specialties and communication styles? Becoming a leader is like stepping into the ring with a brand-new opponent—the game has changed. It's no longer about your individual performance, but how well you can support and guide others to succeed.

Luckily, leadership is less complicated than we make it out to be. At its heart, leadership is a collection of behaviors, *which means it can be learned.*

This is where the Six Functions of a Leader come into play. Yes, effective, performance-optimizing leadership can be boiled down into Six Functions. That doesn't mean mastering leadership is easy, or that every aspect of these Functions is simple, but in these pages awaits a blueprint that can, and will, help you find and home in on your superpower and transform your approach to leadership.

The key objective of a leader is to ensure that those they lead discover their full potential and accomplish goals in a repeatable, sustainable, and optimal way. The Six Functions will provide you with the tools to diagnose any situation and select the best strategies that address real issues. Each Function has its own origin story and purpose, and together they unlock what it means to be a true leader.

Consider this your transformative journey. Perhaps you recently stepped into a formal people-leader role or have been a manager for a few years. Your leadership journey entails self-discovery and learning. It isn't about doing more; it's about doing things differently.

Leadership, like heroism, is built on intentional actions that make a real impact. In the pages that follow, we will chart the course from potential to proficiency, delving into the essence of leadership that goes beyond theory and into practice. All in pursuit of the leader within.

MY ORIGIN STORY

Writing this book has been both my passion and obsession, driven by a deep desire to redefine conventional leadership theories into practical actions. Throughout my career, I've been privileged to work alongside leaders and guide them as they strive to carve out their own unique path to success. Leadership, to me, is an art meant to be accessible and relatable to everyone. It's not an exclusive club reserved for a select few but an endeavor that anyone with desire, the right intent, and the appropriate tools can succeed at.

Having trained and coached countless leaders, I've gained unique insights into the complexities and rewards of true leadership. It's these observations that I'm excited to share with you.

Everyone's leadership journey is their own. Mine had humble beginnings, to say the least.

My first "real" job was in sales at a Holiday Inn hotel. I was responsible for selling to the corporate market, which meant contracting with organizations to use our hotel for overnight stays and meetings. I rocked that job! I met and exceeded my quota regularly. My performance caught the attention of senior leadership, and when my manager left, I was promoted to her role. Imagine my excitement—at the age of twenty-five, I was a manager with a team of people!

My mandate was simple: "Make other sales reps do what you do." Excited and eager to impart my wisdom to my new team, I did the first thing necessary: I went shopping! Don't judge me; for some reason, this was the first place my brain went to—I needed to look the part. Feeling sharp in my new pencil skirt and black high heels, I confidently sailed into the office for my first team meeting.

I seated myself at the head of the table and walked through the agenda I had carefully prepared, but I couldn't help but notice I was met with expressions of indifference and restlessness. The air was thick with silent resistance, killing my enthusiasm and confidence. I couldn't believe it. I was their manager! Why weren't they taking me seriously? I realized at that moment that my position and previous success were not enough.

Somewhere along the way, I had read that being a good role model was the foundation of good leadership. So, I decided to lead by example. I thought if I continued to excel in sales, securing impressive contracts for the hotel, that would inspire the team to do the same. However, my role as a manager required more than just selling. Now, I had tons of internal meetings, including strategy, planning, budgeting, and forecasting. The additional responsibilities piled up. Each day, I was the first person in the office and the last to leave.

I found myself burning out, and yet, this failed to drive my team's results. Later in my career, I learned that this situation happens often. Employees are often promoted into management roles because they are good at their jobs, but the skills that earned them the promotion do not equip them to succeed in leadership.

As I tried to find my own pattern of success as a leader, I immersed myself in everything leadership: I read books, conducted research, attended conferences, and sought out mentors in hopes of learning best practices. I tested each method through trial and error, slowly carving out my own approach. This led me to successful leadership roles at several companies, including Hilton Hotels, where I headed up the hotel's revenue function for ten years.

Over time, I felt a growing motivation to share my knowledge and experiences more broadly. This passion led me to take a leap of faith: starting my own leadership training and development firm. It took me two years to convince my husband that we wouldn't live in a ditch; I knew that I could always find a job somewhere if this didn't pan out. I went back to school and earned a diploma in adult education on top of my business degree and registered my company, Full Circle Connections Inc.

The transition wasn't easy, and there were plenty of ups and downs. The usual trepidations of starting a business and questioning one's abilities to make a go of it were compounded by the personal losses associated with the initial phases of such a drastic change. Working in the hotel business at my level came with some nice perks, like suites and VIP treatment—the full red carpet experience. One day after starting Full Circle Connections, my son, who was in grade school, asked, "Mom, are we ever going to stay in suites again?" I didn't know if we would or not, and it didn't matter to me because, for the first time in my life, I understood what it meant to know your purpose and what it felt like to live it. I understood that I had found my passion.

Helping people find their inner leader within is my purpose.

YOUR TURN

Over the past twenty years, Full Circle Connections has trained thousands of leaders and collaborated with hundreds of successful organizations. This book continues that mission, providing leaders like you with a tool kit to navigate and excel in today's modern, dynamic environment.

Whether you're an aspiring leader or an experienced one, my hope is that this book's practical strategies and actionable insights will help you uncover your own unique leadership style and inspire you to lead with confidence, authenticity, and effectiveness.

Thank you for joining me on this journey as we explore the art of leadership together, unlocking the potential within ourselves and those we lead. Let's redefine what it means to be a leader in today's world, making it a more inclusive, accessible, and fulfilling experience for everyone.

Chapter One

MODERN LEADERSHIP

"The illiterate of the 21st century will not be those who cannot read and write, but those who cannot learn, unlearn, and relearn."

—ALVIN TOFFLER

Several years back, a prominent television network hired Rose to oversee the network's transition to digital broadcasting. When she came on board, she found that her predecessor's lack of vision and direction had left the team exhausted and frustrated. They'd been spinning their wheels without gaining any traction. This caused them to become skeptical and toxic.

Rose acted quickly by outlining a very compelling vision for the future, which was exactly what her team needed to hear. She clarified the network's goals and recognized her team for the work they did. Her tactics fueled everyone, made them feel capable, and lifted their spirits. Rose saw the positive impact her approach had on the team. She continued to reinforce the vision and direction to keep the momentum going.

After a couple of months, however, she began to notice the same dynamics—skepticism, slow progress, and toxicity that surfaced in communications and interactions. She strengthened her message about the vision for the future and reiterated her trust in the team's ability to achieve the goal. Although the words were still powerful and motivating, they did not change how the team felt. Her team needed more than just a vision—they needed clear priorities, defined responsibilities, and new ways to collaborate.

Rose's reliance on her visionary approach, which had previously served her well, became a limitation. Her team lacked a plan to achieve the vision, needed to build new relationships, and required skill development, especially in digital expertise. Her intent was positive—to empower and build accountability—but it's not what the team needed. Her team was floundering, and her efforts weren't making things better.

As you'll discover in the coming chapters, effective leaders embody and execute *Six* Functions, and defining vision is only one of them. Unlocking your leader superpowers requires mastering all six.

Before we look at each of these Functions, however, we need to pause and consider a bigger question: *What is leadership?* Or more specifically, what does it mean to be a *good* leader? If someone like Rose can struggle despite doing good things, it can happen to all of us. In this chapter, we'll pull back the leadership curtain and discuss the mindset the modern leader must adopt to succeed today.

WHAT *IS* LEADERSHIP?

In a recent leadership training workshop with new managers across various functions, I conducted a thought-provoking exercise: *channel wisdom from your role model and answer the question*, "What attributes make a good leader?" Their responses—*visionary, inspiring, honest, transparent, confident, authentic, risk-taker, trusting, caring*, and *empowering*—sparked high energy in the room, creating an electrifying sense of pride in what it means to be a leader.

Immersed in these positive vibes, I playfully said to the group, "That's it! That's leadership. My work here is done." The room fell into momentary silence, the kind that happens when the brain is resolving dissonance.

This scenario highlighted a common dilemma: while we often understand leadership as a theory, we don't always know how to translate these qualities into practice.

Leadership is not about traits alone—it's about action. The essence of leadership is not merely a title or role but the influence you wield in your environment and with the people around you. It's about inspiring and motivating others, guiding them on a path of growth so they can realize their full potential.

True leaders are outcome oriented and avoid grandiose proclamations about their capabilities. They seek concrete evidence of their effectiveness. Instead of proclaiming themselves inspirational, they critically assess whether their team feels inspired. Rather than simply claiming to empower others, they reflect on who has been uplifted by their actions and in what ways. Visionary leaders do more than self-identify; they ensure their team is clear about the direction.

The best leaders understand that their greatest contribution is a world made better by their intentional and purposeful actions.

ADAPTING TO NEW REALITIES

Granted, understanding the most intentional, purposeful actions has become more challenging. The rise of AI is reshaping industries, necessitating leaders at every level to cultivate strategic foresight and decisive agility while managing an overwhelming amount of information. At the same time, organizations are moving toward a decentralized model, empowering employees to contribute more significantly to decision-making, a transition that is creating a set of new expectations for leaders.

Just as superheroes must adapt to new threats, emerging opportunities, and evolving landscapes, so must a leader. Being an effective leader today requires learning new approaches and, perhaps even more importantly, unlearning outdated ones. It's time to let go of the beliefs, mindsets, or practices that may have worked well in the past but now can hinder progress, and embrace a new way of leading that makes the most of the time you already invest in your team.

UNLEARNING LIMITING BELIEFS

An old, wise professor sought a Zen master to learn the essence of wisdom and life's truth. As they sat in a picturesque garden, the master prepared tea, a common ritual to accompany thoughtful dialogue.

As they began to discuss the nature of knowledge and learning, the master, with a gentle hand, poured tea into the visitor's cup. However, he did not stop pouring when the tea reached the brim. Tea began to overflow, spilling down the sides of the cup and onto the table. The professor watched in shock and alarm, and when he could no longer restrain himself, he blurted out, "Stop, the cup is full! No more will fit."

The Zen master paused, allowing the moment to settle.

"Like this cup," he said, "your mind is so filled with your own opinions that it cannot take in anything new. To truly absorb the depth of what you seek, you must first be willing to 'empty your cup.' Only with openness can you truly learn and grow."

This encounter serves as a powerful lesson: the path to wisdom requires humility and the readiness to let go of one's certainty, making space for new insights and understanding.

What beliefs do you hold that may be limiting your ability to lead effectively? Here are seven common ones that may no longer serve in your current environment.

LIMITING BELIEF #1: "LEADERSHIP IS SOMETHING YOU'RE BORN WITH."

There is no such thing as a leadership gene. Leadership is a learned skill, accessible to anyone willing to grow. When I first stepped into leadership, I had to learn everything from scratch—just like everyone else. It's a conscious choice, not a birthright.

LIMITING BELIEF #2: "GOOD LEADERS ARE EXTROVERTS."

Leadership comes in many forms, including from those who are introverted. The key is authenticity, not conforming to stereotypes. Nelson Mandela and Warren Buffett—quiet yet powerful leaders who leveraged their authenticity to inspire change.

LIMITING BELIEF #3: "POSITION DETERMINES LEADERSHIP."

Titles don't make leaders—actions do. Leadership can happen at every level. Think of the times you've leaned on someone for guidance who wasn't your manager. Leadership is about influence, not hierarchy.

LIMITING BELIEF #4: "LEADERS MUST MASTER TECHNICAL SKILLS."

While technical know-how is important, leadership is more about vision and empowerment than mastery of every detail. Leaders need to know when to pull back their knowledge and let others find their own ways to success.

LIMITING BELIEF #5: "MANAGEMENT AND LEADERSHIP ARE THE SAME THING."

Leadership is about vision, direction, and growth; management is about execution and efficiency. Both are necessary, but they're not the same. A good leader balances strategic planning with ensuring that day-to-day operations run smoothly, knowing when to lead and when to manage.

LIMITING BELIEF #6: "LEADERS SHOULD ALWAYS PUT ON AN OPTIMISTIC FRONT."

Blind optimism can be dangerous. True leaders balance hope with honesty and action. During tough times, rather than brushing off concerns, the most effective leaders acknowledge challenges and work with their teams to find a path forward.

So we've busted a few leadership myths. Hopefully, you've emptied some of your teacup and made space for a more intentional approach to leadership—one that isn't about simply doing more but about doing the right things in the right way. In a fast-paced world, this might sound counterintuitive, but the most effective leaders understand that slowing down is often the key to moving forward.

GO SLOW TO GO FAST

I get so much pushback from leaders when I introduce this concept. They tell me they don't have the luxury of slowing down because their world doesn't operate that way. "There's too much to do," they say, "and not enough time to do it." I get it—the pressure is real.

But here's the paradox: the faster we move, the more likely we are to trip ourselves up, making the journey to the desired outcome longer and less efficient. Leadership today isn't about keeping up with the pace of change—that's the baseline; it's about navigating complexity with clarity and purpose. Without thoughtful action, leaders can end up in a loop of recurring challenges, repetitive conversations, and unresolved issues. This constant back-and-forth—clarifying things, realigning the team, and managing the fallout—can build up frustration, erode trust, and take up unnecessary time.

Intentional Leadership isn't about doing more but focusing on what truly matters. But sometimes it's hard to cut through the noise of what truly matters. That's why I developed a simple framework revolving around three key pillars: self-awareness, situational awareness, and intentional action.

To illustrate the pillars, let me share an example from my work with a startup.

A new director of product asked me if I offered time management courses. I said yes, although I rarely do standalone programs that are not connected with a greater strategy. To better understand the root cause of this request, I then asked some questions:

Question: What is driving your need for the time management program?

Answer: Team members not utilizing their time effectively. They are busy, but the right things are not done. We need to drive results and are under a lot of pressure to move faster.

Question: How does your team prioritize their work now?

Answer: I don't know if they prioritize at all. There are so many urgent demands that important tasks may get lost. Our team is pulled in many directions, and the immediate demands overshadow long-term strategic objectives.

Question: How do you communicate the strategic direction for the team? Do you have a vision?

Answer: For the team? No. We have our organizational strategies and goals. They know what to do. We conduct weekly meetings where everyone gives updates on their progress and shares their challenges.

Question: Would you say the issue is more with knowing priorities and less with managing time?

Answer: Well, yes, it appears to be.

This is not an unusual scenario. The leader sees a problem and jumps to conclusions about the root cause—in this case, lack of time management. However, the real issue was an absence of clear vision and unclear priorities. Imagine if we did a time management workshop for that team! It would be a waste of time and money, and more importantly, it would make the team feel misunderstood and undervalued, resulting in resentment and a disconnect between them and the leader.

Intentional Leadership is not about acting but about taking the *right* action based on a thorough understanding of the problem. This ensures solutions are strategic and impactful, leading to improved team performance, enhanced morale, achievement of results, and stronger leader-team relationships.

Let's look at each of the Intentional Leadership pillars in detail.

PILLAR ONE: SELF-AWARENESS

Self-awareness is the leader's ability to recognize and understand their own emotions, strengths, and weaknesses, as well as their influence on others. They need to see their own blind spots and understand how their actions land with others. This self-knowledge shapes how a leader perceives situations and forms the basis for their decisions. Of course, self-awareness is also the starting point of personal growth.

In the director of product example, he needed to reflect on his communication about the team's goals and priorities. He would have been helped by considering questions like, "Have I clearly communicated the direction?" "Do team members understand how their work links with the organizational strategy?" and "How clear am I when it comes to our direction?" If the leader is unclear about the direction, rest assured everyone else is too.

If he had taken time to reflect, the director could have noticed communication gaps and addressed the root causes. This might have involved adjusting his communication style, being more direct, or allowing more room for questions. Recognizing biases, such as assuming the issue was time management, is key in addressing the real problem.

Self-Awareness in Practice

New leaders often ask me: "What is the first thing I should focus on?" My answer is always the same: "Get to know yourself." Develop a clear understanding of how you show up, how others see you, and what drives your communication style and decision-making.

Leaders are not usually eager to listen to this advice. They want quick tips and tactics, but the truth is that no strategy will work if you don't understand the starting point—yourself.

Most of my leadership development training begins with understanding self-awareness, and although there may be initial resistance, the value of knowing oneself becomes clear very quickly. Participants who attend my workshops often comment, with delight, on the first day of training, "I didn't know this would be a therapy session!"

So, how do you create self-awareness? This is not a simple one-and-done exercise. It's an ongoing process because we change and circumstances shift, so we must continuously reassess and recalibrate. There are many proven tools that can be used. (Here come the tips and techniques!)

Feedback

Effective feedback is a powerful tool for building self-awareness and improving leadership effectiveness. There are many ways to gather this information. Some leaders send their teams surveys or conduct quick pulse checks. For more meaningful feedback, consider asking specific questions that go beyond the usual "Do you have any feedback for me?" These can be explored in one-on-one meetings or team discussions. Try asking questions like:

- How can I better support you in your role?
- What leader in the organization do you admire and why?
- What do you miss about your previous manager?
- What advice do you have for me?
- What would have made the last team meeting more productive?
- What is one thing I could change about my leadership style that would help the team perform better?
- How can I improve in providing you with constructive feedback and recognition?
- What is one thing you wish I would start, stop, or continue doing?

These examples are just brainfood. Tailor your questions to reflect your unique reality. The goal is to uncover how your approach is resonating with your team.

Observation

A lot can be learned by simply observing. You might notice that certain conversations end in a predictable, unproductive place. Examine your role in these outcomes: Are you jumping in too quickly with advice, or maybe failing to clarify expectations or priorities?

Clients occasionally ask me to sit in as an observer during their team meeting to give feedback on how it can be improved. The common issue I see is that the meeting belongs to and revolves around the leader. They manage the agenda and drive conversation, stopping momentarily to ask the very thought-provoking, "Any questions?" When someone challenges an issue, the leader responds defensively or launches into overly detailed explanations—after all, it's their agenda, right?

If you find yourself facing similar challenges, take a moment to create space and reflect. Your well-intentioned behaviors might be contributing to the problem. Try switching things up: delegate meeting ownership to someone else, ask more open-ended questions, or simply resist the urge to fill every silence with your voice. By stepping back, you allow others to step forward, which can lead to richer discussions and more productive outcomes.

Psychometric Assessments

Psychometric tests provide quantitative data on various psychological aspects, offering more objective insight into one's strengths and weaknesses. They measure mental traits, abilities, and processes and play a significant role in enhancing self-awareness by offering insight into one's personality, cognitive abilities, emotional intelligence, motivators, and more. Taking these assessments is one of the fastest and best ways to understand yourself.

My favorites, and the ones I use the most in my practice, include the following: our own—Six Functions of a Leader, Full Circle Connections—Everything DiSC by Wiley; The Five Behaviors Team Development by Wiley, based on the bestseller *The Five Dysfunctions of a Team* by Patrick Lencioni; *Working Genius* by Patrick Lencioni; Myers-Briggs Type Indicator; and *Multiplier* by Liz Wiseman. But there are many others. The most important thing to consider is what you're trying to get out of the tools. For example, if you are looking to get insights into your leadership style, you might want to use Everything DiSC to identify whether you are more results-driven or people-oriented and adjust your style accordingly.

A few words of caution: There are many different assessments available. Be mindful and do your research. Some tools, like the free ones out there, can be manipulated and may give you the wrong information. They need to be validated. Ask peers for their experiences using different tools, or try them yourself to see if you trust the results. In addition, while psychometrics can significantly enhance self-awareness, they must be approached with an understanding of their limitations and the context of an individual's unique experiences and circumstances. They offer information captured in a moment in time that is influenced by how the test-taker answered the questions. On another day or in a different mood, the individual may have answered some questions differently, leading to different results.

Whatever tools you use, take the time to understand yourself. A deep comprehension of your strengths, weaknesses, and interests not only helps you understand why you behave the way you do, but also shapes how you perceive the world around you. Recognizing your biases and limitations helps you accurately interpret your environment.

In later chapters, we will explore how personality assessment can be used by leaders in everything from setting expectations to motivating to understanding a team's dynamics.

PILLAR TWO: SITUATIONAL AWARENESS

The second pillar, situational awareness, is what I often refer to as environmental understanding. It's about the leader's ability to accurately perceive the information, events, and dynamics around them, interpret those details in context, and understand how they will impact the team, goals, and overall environment.

For leaders, this means being in tune with the nuances of your team's behavior, the underlying currents in conversations, and the broader organizational and industry landscape. It's about connecting the dots between what's happening and what *could* happen so you can guide your team more effectively.

So how could the director of product in our example leverage situational awareness? Well, for one, he could have reflected on why certain tasks were not actioned and others were overengineered. He could have asked things like, "How does this work align with our overarching goals?" "What speed bumps do you encounter?" "If you had more time, what would you work on?" and "If you had a magic wand, what would you make happen? Why?"

I encourage leaders to develop a dual-track mindset when interacting with others and focus on two aspects of the conversation: (1) what the conversation is about and (2) how the conversation is unfolding.

To do this, you need to occasionally zoom out from the task at hand and observe the other person's reactions. Are they "in the conversation"? Do they seem engaged, puzzled, or unsure? If there's an incongruence between what they say and their tone or body language, stop the conversation and get curious about it. Ask questions like, "How do you feel about what I've said?" "What might be some of your concerns?" "What will the team struggle with?" and "What would help you?" Take the time to gain situational awareness so the actions you take will support and solve the right issues.

Take Lori, who leads a diverse marketing team. She noticed her team's morale and productivity slipping under the pressure of an upcoming high-profile campaign. Reflecting on the situation, Lori realized that in her own stress, she'd been too focused on deadlines and tasks, missing the team's need for support and encouragement. With this newfound awareness, Lori adjusted her approach, becoming more supportive, empathetic, and communicative to help ease the tension her team was feeling.

Lori also observed that the high-pressure environment was exacerbating communication breakdowns, creating conflict and silos within the team. In response, she organized a workshop to help the team build resilience, learn solid prioritization practices, and strengthen cohesion. Additionally, she implemented weekly check-ins to provide a platform for open discussion and collaborative problem-solving.

Driven by self-awareness and situational awareness, Lori's actions to recalibrate her leadership approach led to the desired result. The workshop and meetings enhanced understanding and communication among members and rebuilt the team's morale.

PILLAR THREE: INTENTIONAL ACTION

Finally, intentional action represents the culmination of self-awareness and situational awareness insights that move into tangible outcomes. It involves making informed, confident decisions and acting upon them with purpose and responsibility. The action is intentional because the leader knows precisely what problem they are solving and what outcome they are looking for.

Too often, leaders get caught up in the urgency of tasks, mistaking speed for true efficiency. To be effective, you must resist the urge to jump into action without a pause for reflection. Always interrogate the purpose behind the action. What problem is it solving? What outcomes will I get? Slowing down like this will enable you to go fast in the long run.

YOUR MISSION

Your mission as a leader is straightforward: to elevate and capture the full potential in people and situations. Leadership is not only about the paths you choose or the decisions you make; it's about ensuring those paths and decisions illuminate the strengths of those you guide, fostering environments where optimal outcomes can naturally emerge.

Just as Alvin Toffler suggested, today's leaders must learn, unlearn, and relearn. Modern leadership demands that we slow down enough to move forward with greater clarity, purpose, and velocity.

When Rose refused to reassess her definition of leadership, she unknowingly trapped her team in a cycle of inaction and frustration. By practicing self-awareness, situational awareness, and intentional action, you can avoid those same pitfalls and choose a different path—one that's rooted in understanding, strategy, and effective execution.

As we've already said, leadership can be learned. That's the beauty of a skill set based entirely on intentional, purposeful actions—the Six Functions. Let's dive into those Functions, their purpose, their use, and how they came to exist.

Chapter Two

THE SIX FUNCTIONS
OF A LEADER

"If you define the problem correctly, you almost have the solution."

—STEVE JOBS

The dictionary defines a "function" as "any of a group of related actions contributing to a larger action" or "the action for which a person or thing is specially fitted or used or for which a thing exists."[1] Quite a mouthful, but the essence is simple: functions enable us to get shit done.

This chapter is a beginner's guide to the Six Functions and how these enable leaders to drive meaningful results through intentional leadership. By learning how the Functions evolved through real-world challenges and the purpose they serve, you will gain a better understanding of how all six come together

---

1   *Merriam-Webster Dictionary*, "function," accessed December 5, 2024, https://www.merriam-webster.com/dictionary/function.

to diagnose issues, strategize for improvement, and enable you to lead more effectively.

THE SIX FUNCTIONS MODEL

The Six Functions help simplify the complex task of leadership by translating theory and concepts into actionable steps, all in pursuit of one vision: realizing the full potential of individuals and teams.

The Six Functions of a Leader framework is distilled from over two decades of working with leaders and organizations across diverse industries.

The Framework:

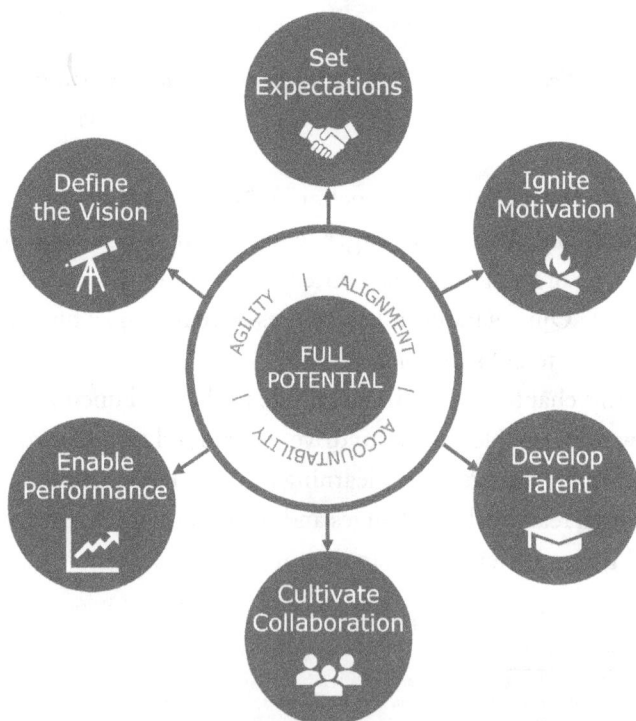

I'll unpack the Six Functions individually in the chapters that follow. For now, here is a brief overview:

- **Define the Vision:** Guides your team with a clear direction and purpose, ensuring that everyone understands and aligns the long-term goals and the collective mission.
- **Set Expectations:** Establishes clear goals and priorities that support success, aligning team efforts with organizational objectives and providing clarity on what needs to be achieved.
- **Ignite Motivation:** Fuels passion and deep commitment within the team, creating engagement and energy that drive performance.
- **Develop Talent:** Builds competencies and prepares employees for current and future challenges, fostering continuous growth and innovation to sustain performance.
- **Cultivate Collaboration:** Fosters strong connections within teams and taps into diverse perspectives, driving creativity and execution to achieve better results.
- **Enable Performance:** Optimizes results through ongoing coaching, mentoring, and feedback, continuously improving performance and maintaining high standards.

The Six Functions serve as a diagnostic tool, sharpening situational awareness. When faced with challenges, analyzing which Function to focus on helps identify the root cause. Perhaps it's a lack of motivation, poor morale, or ineffective teamwork. The framework acts as a lens to assess the issues and offers targeted strategies to address them.

With its own set of unique skills, each Function equips leaders with the tools they need to address specific challenges, providing actionable strategies tailored to the situation. By mastering these skills, leaders pave the way for their teams to realize their true potential.

That is why in the center of the Six Functions model is full potential—not just for the organization, but for the individuals who share their lives and talents with it. Leaders achieve results by creating environments where people feel valued, supported, and inspired to grow. When employees feel safe and engaged, they're more likely to tap into their own potential, leading to better outcomes for everyone.

When leaders effectively navigate the Six Functions, they create outcomes that drive results: *agility*, *alignment*, and *accountability*. These aren't just abstract concepts but essential elements that empower individuals and teams to adapt quickly, focus on shared goals, and take ownership of their contributions, unlocking the full potential within teams. Each element plays a distinct role, and together they form a foundation for sustainable success.

- **Agility:** When changes, challenges, and opportunities come up, agility helps people respond quickly and effectively. It's about being open, flexible, and adaptable so uncertainty doesn't stall progress.
- **Alignment:** This is about synchronizing efforts with the broader team or organizational strategy. Alignment creates focus, enables better decision-making, and allows for coordinated and efficient progress toward shared objectives.
- **Accountability:** When you create a culture where people are responsible for their actions and performance, they learn to take ownership. When everyone feels accountable, they're more likely to contribute positively and ensure the entire team succeeds.

Can you imagine leading a team that has all these ingredients? Sounds like utopia? Well, it's doable. Many of my clients have found their way through the Six Functions. Think of them as your own yellow brick road, guiding you and your team toward success. And just like Dorothy (not me, the OZ one!), you might discover you've had the superpower all along—no red slippers required, just Intentional Leadership!

BIRTH OF THE FUNCTIONS

The first question I'm often asked is why six? Why not five, ten, or any other number? The truth is, the Six Functions were not the result of a deliberate count but an organic progression. They didn't appear fully formed, as if etched in stone next to a burning bush; they evolved through continuous adaptation to the ebb and flow of economic and societal shifts.

The first Function, Ignite Motivation, crystallized during the 2008 financial crisis, a time of significant upheaval where companies faced downsizing and strategic redirection. This era saw employees grappling with disillusionment and fear, which in turn impacted their performance. The correlation between employee engagement and productivity became apparent, and engagement surveys revealed a critical gap in leadership. As I worked through this challenge with my clients, it became clear that what employees needed most was an intrinsic connection—to their work, to their company's mission, and to a sense of shared purpose.

The second Function, Define the Vision, also had a clear inception. I collaborated with a startup that had just secured Series B funding. The CEO was a brilliant innovator, but the company's focus and priorities were scattered. Despite the influx of capital, they struggled to develop and release new products on time. Leaders diligently put in time to manage performance—setting expectations, providing feedback, and coaching—yet saw little traction. It wasn't that employees lacked dedication or effort; their actions were simply misaligned with the company's overarching goals. Once we defined and communicated a compelling vision and a clear direction, every project and task became a stepping stone toward the shared objectives.

I am not sure which Function followed, but the order doesn't matter. Recurring themes emerged over the years through needs analysis and direct experience with clients. Despite the varying pain points my clients faced, the root causes were strikingly similar. Issues like lack of vision, unclear expectations, disengagement, no skills or growth, inability to collaborate, and poor performance were consistent. I stopped trying to re-create or find fault with the six critical areas of leadership and leaned in to better understand them, creating models and frameworks that give leaders the necessary tools to navigate each Function effectively.

THE REAL TEST

The acid test of this framework's value came in March 2020. The pandemic, which began as a distant headline, was suddenly at our doorstep, disrupting lives and businesses in ways we could have never imagined. Offices emptied in haste, leaving leaders and teams in the throes of a frightening new normal. Like many, I found myself at a crossroads, facing the uncertain fate of my practice, which had thrived for seventeen years.

Overwhelmed with doubt, I considered closing my company. I wasn't sure I could transition to a virtual format. Truthfully, I didn't really know what that would entail.

In a moment, tinged with the warmth of a wine-induced glow, I had a thought: If I wasn't sure what to do next, how must my clients feel? The leaders I trained, coached, and helped on their journeys—what were they feeling, and what did they need? Helping others and being of service have always been my drive and passion, and this situation was no different.

I turned to the Six Functions framework and reflected on what employees needed from their leaders and organizations at that moment. Overnight, I created two virtual training programs—one for Set Expectations and another for Cultivate Collaboration.

The first program tackled the immediate questions facing employees—how to adapt their work hours to new realities, manage professional responsibilities alongside personal ones like childcare or sharing an office with a partner, and prioritize tasks when the business landscape was shifting daily. The second program was designed to redefine teamwork in a remote setting. It focused on reimagining meetings and collaboration techniques, ensuring that distance didn't become a barrier to productivity and innovation.

With renewed energy and purpose, I emailed my clients to let them know about the new programs. Bookings came, partly because my clients were desperate for some direction but also because some felt bad for me and wanted to be supportive. No matter the motivation, the results were spectacular. Feedback from leaders was that they had newfound confidence and clarity on their priorities. They knew what their people needed and how to engage in conversations with their direct reports in a way that addressed real needs. My inbox filled with messages of gratitude and more business.

As the remote world continued, new Functions became essential. After a few months of lockdowns, Ignite Motivation took center stage as people began to burn out. The stress of working in isolation and managing work-life balance started to take its toll, performance began to slip, and leaders began to feel more like therapists than managers. That's when the Enable Performance Function became a priority. Leaders needed to find a balance between being supportive and achieving results.

The events of this time crystallized the value of the Six Functions. It was not a theoretical construct but a vital, real-world lifeline. The Functions became a tool that helped me, and other leaders, define the problem correctly, creating insight and recognition that targeted real issues.

LEADERSHIP VERSATILITY

As we discussed, leadership is about intentional, focused, and deliberate behaviors that unlock the full potential in others. The Six Functions serve as a compass, providing clear strategies to address various situations. They are not meant to be applied in a sequential order and are not to be used all at once. Instead, they serve as a tool kit for leaders to operate within the three pillars, by gaining self-awareness, becoming aware of the situation—the team's needs—and engaging in intentional action by selecting the most effective strategy.

For example, consider a new cross-functional team starting a fresh project. They are unfamiliar with each other's working styles and unsure of where to start. In this scenario, the strategies under Cultivate Collaboration would be most useful. Let's say the same team, further along in the project, begins to miss milestones. It might be necessary to explore the actions in Set Expectations or Enable Performance to realign efforts with objectives.

Before the Six Functions can be mastered, leaders will find it helpful to identify any natural affinity toward certain Functions.

Our personality preferences and current needs often draw us to specific Functions over others.

Remember Rose, our television executive? Her natural inclination was to lead with vision, which initially worked well and showed positive results. Unfortunately, Rose didn't recognize the need to shift her approach, which led to more skepticism and toxicity on her team.

Rose's experience highlights a common pitfall: when a strategy works once, leaders may over-rely on it, hoping for continued success despite clear evidence that it is no longer working. As Einstein famously said, "Insanity is doing the same thing over and over and expecting different results." Understanding yourself allows you to flex to the situation and people's needs.

PATHWAY TO MASTERY

So, let's get started. Each of the following chapters focuses on one function, guiding you through the "what," "why," and "how" trajectory toward mastery—*what* each function entails, *why* it's important, and *how* to apply it effectively.

Like Steve Jobs said, "If you define the problem correctly, you almost have the solution." The Six Functions will help you do just that: clearly define the challenges you face and provide actionable solutions that will empower you to lead with confidence.

The purpose of these chapters is not just to explain the inner workings of each Function and why they play an important role in the development of effective leadership practices. They also provide hands-on tools you can refer back to throughout your leadership journey, making this a practical guide for modern leaders.

Simple, uncomplicated leadership—achieving one vision with Six Functions.

---------- *Chapter Three* ----------

DEFINE THE VISION

"A team without direction is like a ship without a compass. It may move, but it won't reach its destination."

If you're thinking about skipping this chapter because your company already has a vision, don't. I'm not talking about a corporate vision. While it's true that corporate vision is incredibly important and sets the overarching strategy, it's the unique visions of individual teams that make those strategies a reality.

Think of the corporate vision as the destination on a map, a place everyone is aiming to reach. Each team is like a separate vessel navigating its own waters to the common point. Without a unique charted path, teams can lose their way in the vast oceans of daily operations.

Sometimes, the broader organizational vision may lack relevance or fail to inspire every team member. If you work in procurement for a travel company, how do you plug into a vision that says, "We aim to help families enjoy the experience of traveling together"? The connection between the vision and the work may feel disjointed. Likewise, the company vision that talks about changing the world through innovation may be relevant to someone who works in product development but is completely devoid of meaning for accounts receivable.

Call it whatever you'd like—vision, purpose, direction—teams need a common goal to rally around, one that clarifies priorities and creates alignment, commitment, and a sense of belonging. Defining a vision for your team is not just a box to be checked but a living, inspiring force that gives meaning to work, empowers decision-making, and supports a strong team culture.

I intentionally titled the Function *Define* the Vision and not *Set* the Vision. There is a subtle but important distinction. From my perspective, setting the vision involves deciding on the ultimate goal or end state the team aims to reach. Setting is actually part of defining and is a necessary first step.

Defining the vision, on the other hand, gives the goal clarity and depth. We need to know the destination (setting), but we also need to understand the value of reaching it and the journey of getting there (defining).

Your team's vision is a lighthouse, cutting through the fog of daily operations. Without it, your team might keep moving, but drift off course. With a clear vision, they're guided toward the destination with confidence, avoiding the rocks that could derail their progress.

WHY DEFINE THE VISION?

A strong team vision aligns all team members toward common goals and priorities. It motivates the team by giving their work meaning, showing them how their efforts contribute to the bigger picture, and fosters a sense of belonging.

A well-defined vision also supports decision-making by

acting as a filter, ensuring all actions are aligned with team objectives, and drives commitment by engaging team members so they feel invested in the team's success. Additionally, it facilitates communication with a common language for discussing progress and challenges, and encourages innovation by setting a clear destination that allows for creative problem-solving.

Of the Six Functions, this is the one that I spend the most time convincing leaders to focus on. Our workplaces are so fixated on getting things done that we rush to the doing and often don't stop and think about the bigger picture. This chapter is your call to slow down, determine whether your team's vision needs defining, and take steps to craft one that inspires each team member to reach their full potential.

YEARNING FOR VISION AND INSPO

The Leadership Challenge, a book written by James Kouzes and Barry Posner, is a guide to becoming the kind of leader that other people want to follow. In the authors' research of over four hundred thousand people worldwide, four characteristics of a great leader are identified:

1. *Honesty:* This is considered a personal quality more than a professional one. When leaders openly communicate their thoughts, intentions, and challenges, they are more relatable and authentic, people whom others can respect and identify with.
2. *Competence:* People want their leader to be capable, effective, and experienced. No one wants to follow someone who may lead them into failure.
3. *Vision:* People want their leaders to have a clear idea of where they are headed. They want them to envision a better future and work toward it rather than merely living with the status quo.

4. *Inspiration:* A leader must be able to communicate the vision in a way that creates passion and belief that what they do will improve lives.

Drawing from the four leadership traits identified by Kouzes and Posner, we see that vision and inspiration are not just desirable attributes but foundational for leadership. A leader's role is not only to define a vision, but also to articulate it compellingly—to inspire.

VISION LEADS, OBJECTIVES FOLLOW

Before we dive in, it's important to note that *vision* and *objectives* are not the same thing. Many of my clients have embraced OKRs (objectives and key results) to set focus and measure performance. Whatever metrics your organization uses, all employees should have their own measurable objectives that are visited regularly. But objectives are not a vision. So often, I hear from leaders, "We have a vision. My team knows where we are going because they have OKRs."

You see, when teams drive toward the direction using tools like OKRs, it's like a tail wagging the dog. You've got the order mixed up. What are the objectives driving toward? What is the desired outcome? Lead with your vision and let the objective follow as the path to the destination.

Let's say you're planning for an upcoming vacation. Perhaps you want to recharge your batteries by being alone in a peaceful and serene island resort. This resort represents your vision—a place where you can relax and de-stress. To get there, you need to book flights, reserve accommodations, and plan activities. These are your objectives.

If you start with booking the flights and planning activities without knowing your desired outcome, you might be swayed by the cheapest flight offer and end up in a bustling city instead, missing out on the relaxation and tranquility you envisioned.

The vision determines where you want to go, while the objectives guide the actions to get you there. Ideally, you filter your team's objectives through the vision by asking questions like:

- How does this objective directly support our vision?
- How will achieving this get the team closer to our team's desired outcome?
- How will this objective add value to the team and the vision?

Imagine how motivating it is for the team to know that each member's objectives go through this process. That there is shared purpose, alignment, and unity. Priceless!

CRAFT OR REFINE?

Here is a quiz to help you decide if your team would benefit from having a vision or revisiting the vision you might already have. Answer yes or no for each:

- My team members are clear about our priorities.
- My team understands how their work aligns with the organizational strategy.
- Our team's purpose is clear and motivating to everyone.
- My team members can articulate our team's vision.
- My team members refer to the vision regularly when making decisions.
- If I ask my team members to tell me about the team's purpose, they'd give me the same answer.

• My people are excited about the work they do.

If you said no to any of these, your team probably needs to think about clarifying an inspirational direction for your team.

THE MAGIC OF DEFINING A VISION

I received this email from a client:

Hi Dorothy,

Nice to e-meet you, I got your name from a colleague of mine who engaged you to work with his team. He said you did magic for his team, and I need some of that magic. I have a team of brilliant individuals who work really hard. They are overwhelmed with the amount of work, and even though they put in a lot of hours, I am not seeing the type of results we need. I am not sure if you can help, but I would love an opportunity to chat with you.

I chose to share this particular email because the reference to magic made me laugh. But this is not an unusual request. After a call with the client, we decided on a one-day offsite to explore the challenges and barriers the team is facing and find opportunities to overcome those.

The workshop began with an icebreaker. I asked each team member to rate on a whiteboard areas of strength and weakness for the team as a whole. Strengths got green dots and weaknesses got red.

On the whiteboard, I listed:

• Well-defined vision
• Clearly defined team priorities

- Roles and responsibilities
- Collaboration
- Resources and tools
- Team communication
- Decision-making

I explained the context of each and asked them to individually go to the whiteboard and vote. Here were the results:

- Well-defined vision: all green except one
- Clearly defined team priorities: all red except one
- Roles and responsibilities: about fifty-fifty
- Collaboration: two green, the rest red
- Resources and tools: two green, the rest red
- Team communication: about fifty-fifty
- Decision-making: all red

After everyone had finished, I asked for their observations, surprises, or confirmations. No one was really surprised by the results. I told them that we would explore each of the elements, focusing on finding solutions for their greatest challenges—prioritization and decision-making.

But, my experience told me that the areas identified as weaknesses were often a symptom of not having a defined vision. To test that, we dove into the vision. I asked the team to each write the answer to this two-part question: "Why do you, as a team, exist? What is your purpose or vision?"

Of course, everyone assumed that because it rated as a strength in the exercise, this would be super easy, and we could get through this part of the offsite meeting quickly. That was far from what actually happened. The team members struggled to capture their collective purpose. It took a long time and some real discomfort for everyone to have something written down. I asked each team member to share their answer, one by one.

To their surprise, the team's views differed—some slightly, some vastly. After everyone shared, I sat down and asked the group to zoom out and reflect on the last fifteen minutes. I didn't need to facilitate this part of the conversation. The team, on their own, came to the realization that the areas they identified as weaknesses were a direct outcome of not having a unified vision. How can a team have common priorities, communicate well, or make solid decisions if there is no anchor?

This is a frequent occurrence. Most teams believe they have a common vision or purpose. That is not exactly false because individuals have their own interpretations of what the vision is and assume that it is shared by everyone. But rarely does a team have a single, solid statement that emerges organically and is so ingrained in their culture that it can be cited at a moment's notice.

If your team has a compelling vision that serves as the North Star and gives meaning and purpose to the work they do, good for you! Keep working at it. Ensure it's at the forefront of discussions. Encourage your direct reports to use it as a filter to make decisions, establish priorities, and reignite motivation.

An HR team I work with does this really well. Their vision statement is, "To unleash the talents of our people through one-of-a-kind employee experience." As a scaling startup, the company is preparing for growth, and of course the possibilities of what systems, policies, and practices to set up are endless. As often happens, everyone has ideas about what the organization needs. When decisions must be made about the right HRIS (human resource information system), for example, the team uses their vision to cut through the noise by asking. "Which system will provide our employees with the best, one-of-a-kind experience?"

I'm often asked *when* a team should define their vision. Well, the obvious answer is now—if you don't have one. If you do, consider whether it needs a revision. Unlike organizational visions, the ones for teams don't have a long shelf life. The exact time one lasts can't be predicted. The world changes so fast; AI may disrupt and shift the direction for a marketing team faster than the operations team, for example. It's important that, as a leader, you build a mindset that the vision is a compass and if team direction changes, so will the destination.

Some visions don't need a complete overhaul; maybe just a word or two needs to be tweaked to realign with current reality. Others will change dramatically over time. There is no right or wrong here as long as the desired end result matches the team's direction.

Some of the most transcendent companies have vision statements that are unrecognizable from their first iterations. For example, here's Apple's statement from the 1980s: "To make a contribution to the world by making tools for the mind that advance humankind." And here's Apple's vision statement today: "To make the best products on earth, and to leave the world better than we found it."

In other situations, a simple tweaking is better than taking a stick of dynamite to the team vision. Here's a statement for a software engineering team in 2017: "We deliver reliable and client-centric solutions." Here's the 2024 statement from the same team: "We develop reliable and cutting-edge solutions that make a meaningful impact."

Some visions do stand the test of time. When I started my own business twenty years ago, I embarked on the process of creating a vision statement. In a book that I wish I remembered the title of, I read about the importance of having such a statement. So, like a good student, I went to work. I found the process to be very arduous. I am not a detail-oriented person by nature, and getting to the other side of having a vision involves wading through some deep thinking and analysis.

I quit many times, but somehow saw enough value in the process to push through. My consulting business was a blank canvas. I was a team of one; the world was my oyster, and I had no idea where to start or, more importantly, where to focus. Later in this chapter, I will share with you the process I went through, but for now, I want to let you know that the vision I created in October 2003 is still the same today. Sometimes, I think about changing it, but it still feels relevant and continues to inspire and fuel me.

My vision statement: "To support people in learning and discovering their paths."

This statement is at the forefront of everything I do (okay, almost everything). I reflect on how every training I design and every coaching session I conduct will help others learn not just skills but about themselves so they can find their path of purpose and lead fulfilling and meaningful lives.

My statement is not just words; it is the core of my business. When I feel overwhelmed and stressed, it is my source of energy. What power! I can't encourage you enough to create a statement with your teams.

If your team has a defined vision but you are not sure if it needs some refinement, the following questions can help. You're not looking for a certain number of yes or no answers. These questions simply provide brainfood to help you consider whether your guiding force needs some work.

- Has the business or competitive environment changed significantly?
- Has the organization shifted?

- Does the vision motivate and inspire?
- Is the vision used to help determine priorities and make decisions?
- Has our team's mandate changed?
- Is the team working well together?

You can also consider areas of tension, blockage, or speed bumps in how work is performed. These are the "What keeps you up at night?" questions.

- Is your team slow at decision-making?
- Are your employees plagued by low energy?
- Are there silos within the team?
- Are your meetings boring, and are issues left unresolved?
- Do your team members willingly take initiative?
- Is there ideation or innovation within your team?

Many of the issues uncovered by asking these questions are rooted in a lack of direction and misalignment. A solid vision can help to move the team forward.

FORMAL ASSESSMENTS TO CREATE SITUATIONAL AWARENESS

As part of our leadership development training, we ask managers to conduct a Six Functions 180-Assessment (direct reports provide feedback for the leader) or a Six Functions 360-Assessment (feedback gathered from the leader's direct reports, peers, and manager). The results provide insights into how effectively the leader navigates through the Six Functions and what the team needs the most.

From over a thousand assessments, the results show a persistent discrepancy: leaders rate their teams very low on the statement, "My team members understand our team's priorities." Yet, their direct reports rate the statement, "I understand my team's priorities" very high.

If you are a manager frustrated with your team's inability to work on the right stuff and to prioritize what really matters, this is probably not a surprise to you. There is a gap between the leader's expectations and the team's perception of reality. This again underscores the necessity of a shared vision, which serves as a cornerstone for aligning focus and ensuring that everyone is not just busy being busy, but busy with purpose.

So, what if you realize your team doesn't have a vision or has one that is in dire need of updating? Then it's time to craft one.

CRAFTING A VISION

Before you get busy ideating and jumping to vision statements, embody the "go slow to go fast" principle. Consider what the best strategy is for creating a clear direction.

SOLO OR COLLECTIVE?

This is the question that should be asked before you do anything else, as its answer serves as the initial guidepost for your envisioning journey.

There is a case for both. Yes, of course, creating the vision with the team's input is the way to go. Involving team members in the development creates a sense of ownership and commitment to achieving it.

However, there are circumstances when collective work isn't ideal, like when the team has a long history together and a lot of baggage, toxicity, and individualistic approaches to getting work done. In these cases, I suggest leaders draft the vision on their own and then spend time with the team refining it and getting buy-in. This approach can be more efficient and establish a fresh starting point for the team to work together.

I once worked with a team at a financial institution that was—there's no other way to put it—a shit show. They'd been together for over a decade and had a turbulent history laced with resentment, grudges, and toxicity. They had gone through four leaders who left without making a dent in improving team dynamics.

When leader number five came into the picture—someone I had worked with at another company—we decided to try building the vision with the whole team. I kicked off our session by getting everyone to agree on the team's reason for existence. The first question I posed was, "Who do you serve?" The answer was unanimous—the customer.

We were on the right track. Next, I asked, "What would be the impact on the customer if this team ceased to exist?"

Answers bounced around a bit, but there was agreement that customers had choices and would leave the bank and go somewhere else. Okay, they had a sense of importance. Great! We talked through how they supported the customer, and although I noticed there was no dialogue between team members, each was very clear about what they did.

After that came the natural question, "How dependent are you on each other to meet your job objectives and provide the best service to the customer?"

This was the tell-tale moment. After a bit of silence, those who spoke up said they weren't dependent on anyone. When I challenged that, certain team members became very vocal about the fact that they didn't need anyone to succeed, had a lot of experience in their respective areas, and working with others stalled progress without adding value. Some stayed quiet and nodded, and others appeared very uncomfortable.

For the rest of the session, I tried a variety of ways to break through the tension, but it was evident that the team's legacy would not allow them to shift their perspectives enough to move forward with creating a common future. We finished that part of the session by acknowledging the uncovered commonalities and moved on to our next topic.

In this case, going solo first was more efficient. The leader drafted the bones of the vision using the commonalities explored by the team, presented it to them, and, together, they worked through the final statement and discussed how the vision could be achieved.

Ultimately, whether you choose a solo or collective approach should depend on the specific dynamics and needs of your team. The goal is to ensure the vision is embraced and effectively implemented.

BUSINESS ACUMEN

Once you answer the solo-versus-collective question, the next step is to consider the broader context of your company's strategic direction. A solid team vision must tie in with the company's big picture, which requires that you as the leader understand how different areas of the business connect. Seeing beyond your slice of the pie allows you to define a meaningful and relevant team destination. It's about knowing how everything clicks together—from sales and marketing to operations and finance.

Senior leaders tend to have higher business acumen. They've

usually been in the game longer, have worked their way up through various roles, and understand that thinking holistically about the organization is a big part of their job. But newer leaders, first- and second-level managers, are naturally more focused on their own area. That can create siloed decision-making, which can impact cross-functional collaboration and lead to groupthink. For example, a marketing team's vision might be to market products effectively to their customers. This team, not understanding the context of the work, might see the product team as an adversary if they're constantly changing direction or not keeping marketing up-to-date on product development.

Reflecting on your knowledge about the business is a great starting point for assessing your own business acumen. Ask yourself these questions to begin the process of developing an action plan for yourself:

- What areas of our business do I understand the least?
- When do I encounter knowledge gaps that impact my effectiveness or efficiency?
- What knowledge would help me to make better, more informed decisions?
- What business skills are holding me back?
- What departments are the most challenging to collaborate with? Why?
- Where do I or my team experience the most tension? Why?

Next, look at your answers for some themes. Did you identify some weaknesses or pain points? These may include areas like departmental budgets, marketing campaigns, revenue streams, regulatory compliance, market understanding, product management, or data analytics.

Now, prioritize these. When everything is important, nothing is important. So, pick the most pressing.

Next, map out a plan for your top priorities. Generate ideas for how you can level up. Keep things simple. Your list could include relatively small actions like finding a mentor, taking an online course, working on a cross-functional project, requesting informal interviews with others, reading books, case studies, and industry reports, attending a conference, or listening to podcasts.

It will always serve you well to build a strong cross-functional network within the organization. Spend time learning and discovering what other areas of the company are working on, their priorities, and their challenges. Building networks is difficult in the hybrid workplace, but it is doable with intention and a strategy. Participate in meetings, involve yourself in special projects, and build connections that expose you to new people and areas of business as much as possible. Being business savvy will not only help you define the vision; it will also help you navigate all Six Functions.

THE VISIONING PROCESS

Now that you've figured out how you will approach crafting the vision, it's time to get into the process itself.

There are many ways to create a vision. The process I use with clients is simple and comprehensive. I call it the "Four Cs of Visioning."

But even though the process is simple, it is not necessarily easy. It requires flexing in different areas to arrive at a meaningful statement. If you are like me and enjoy brainstorming and big picture thinking, you will prefer the first part of the process. If you are like my husband, more analytical and fond of rationalizing each step along the way, you need to brace yourself and manage the discomfort until the ideas are out and can be analyzed and evaluated.

The Four Cs process offers a disciplined approach and involves four steps:

1. **Create:** Brainstorm to gather ideas, discern, prioritize, and craft the draft.
2. **Connect:** Draw links between the draft and the organizational strategy and culture.
3. **Communicate:** Test the vision with stakeholders to ensure clarity and get buy-in.
4. **Cultivate:** Implement the vision and build mechanisms to use it in everyday decision-making and planning.

To help you see how this visioning process works, let's follow one example all the way through, pausing to focus on each of the Cs in turn.

Swift Shift's marketing team was struggling with execution. They worked hard, and although campaigns eventually launched on time, the process leading up to that was stressful and chaotic. The new marketing director, Mia, made it her first priority to remove the barriers to delivery. She believed that providing clarity and direction through a vision would help the team achieve their goals with greater ease.

Mia began the process by gathering her team for a half-day session. She explained the purpose of the work they were about to embark on and how a vision statement would help the team alleviate some stress. Once gathered, the team engaged in an icebreaker to warm up and get to know each other, and then Mia began the process.

Create

Create is the initial step in the visioning process, the first of our Four Cs. During this time, it's important to gather ideas and figure out which ones take priority over others. This is the time to be free and creative while you narrow down those ideas into what will ultimately become a draft of your vision statement. This work is done with the team—or individually if a solo process is more efficient. Here's what that looked like with Swift Shift.

Mia prepared a few questions for the team to work through. She asked one question at a time and used different tools to capture their input.

Question One: What do we do?

She asked everyone to reflect on the question in silence and to capture their answer on a Post-it note. After a couple minutes, she asked each team member to stand and read what they wrote while posting their answer on a blank wall.

After everyone had their turn, she asked the team to discuss differences and similarities. This part of the process surfaced differing thoughts, which, through thorough discussions, led to agreement and alignment on what they do. I often say to leaders, "It's less important what the team says and more important that they say it." To come to a meaningful statement, the team must have and manage some tension during the visioning process.

Question Two: What value do we bring to Swift Shift?

Mia set a timer for seven minutes and asked the group to share their thoughts. While team members spoke, Mia captured key words on the whiteboard. The purpose behind this question was twofold: one, appreciation for the work the team does and, two, to start laying the foundation for envisioning.

Question Three: What are some trends we are seeing in marketing?

Mia divided the team into three groups and asked them to discuss what changes and trends they'd observed. She encouraged them to think outside their industry and to consider their experiences as a customer, whether going to Starbucks or buying a phone. They had ten minutes to discuss and capture the key points to share with the group.

Asking people to think about marketing more broadly is especially effective at getting the team to think outside of their own functional and organizational bubble, which can generate different, more innovative ideas.

Question Four: How do we want to be perceived by our peers and clients?

Mia challenged the team to imagine their ideal reputation within the company and beyond. "Think big," she encouraged, "and consider not just where we are but where we want to be." The team brainstormed and shared their aspirations, which Mia recorded on the whiteboard.

Mia transitioned to test if there was a vision emerging. She encouraged the team to review the whiteboard and share their thoughts. To Mia's pleasant surprise, everyone agreed they could see the vision taking shape. Once again, she broke the team into smaller groups and asked them to write a vision statement for the team on flip charts, encouraging the groups to keep it short—one or two sentences—and not to worry about the words, which could be polished later.

After ten minutes, Mia brought the groups back together to distill their ideas into a clear vision statement. Each team presented their statements and shared their discussions as Mia guided them through identifying common themes and powerful phrases from the notes on the whiteboard. The team debated and discussed, gradually merging their ideas into a succinct sentence that encapsulated their shared aspirations and values. Mia ensured everyone's voice was heard, fostering a sense of ownership and commitment to the emerging vision. The process took twenty minutes.

The vision statement: "We are a creative engine that drives consumer engagement and brand loyalty."

The big difference between an organizational and a team vision is that a team vision does not need to be shared or understood by anyone other than the team. If you choose to share, that's fine, but it can remain a secret code. As long as the team understands the context, the statement provides direction, and the statement is motivating, you can make it whatever it needs to be. Some of the statements I've seen:

- "Drive operational excellence through sustainability."
- "We create kickass campaigns."
- "We unleash the talents of our people."
- "We lead the way in technology excellence."
- "To redefine the way people interact with technology through intuitive and beautiful design."
- "To be a leader in cutting-edge research and innovation in our field."
- "To push the boundaries of knowledge and make groundbreaking discoveries that benefit humanity."

- "We f***** rock and it won't be a secret."

When creating the final statement, using AI can be very helpful, but, there is a big BUT…the team needs to do the work that leads to this step. If you use a tool like ChatGPT, input the outcomes from the team and ask for several suggestions. Work with your people to shape the final statement. Don't skip the entire process of envisioning. To get the full value of defining the vision, the conversation matters.

Connect

After the statement is drafted, it's time to connect it to the organization's strategic direction. A solid vision ties in with the larger strategy. This is where your business savvy comes in!

Warren Bennis hit the nail on the head: "Leadership is the capacity to translate vision into reality." Sometimes, a company can make this easier with a clear plan that's understood and embodied, but if that's not the case for you, dig around until you find that North Star for your team. This could be a mission statement, strategic plan, OKRs, or anything that will act as an anchor.

Now that Mia's team had a statement that seemed to motivate and inspire them, she asked, "How does our statement align with the company's vision: To redefine our sector by offering unparalleled value, sparking deep consumer connections, and cultivating brand advocacy."?

The team didn't struggle with finding a connection between their mission to drive consumer engagement and brand loyalty and the company's overall objective of developing consumer connections and brand advocacy, at which point Mia transitioned to the next step.

Communicate

This step is the testing phase for a vision in development. After drafting it and linking it to the organization's strategic direction, the next step is to identify stakeholders and determine if and how to communicate it to them. This process serves two purposes: gaining clarity among the team regarding what the vision means and why it is important, and then generating buy-in. Everyone involved needs to be sold on the new vision for it to be successful. Thus, communication becomes key.

In Swift Shift's case, Mia asked how the team should test their newly created statement. Who were the key stakeholders, and should the team share this vision with them for input?

The team agreed that they would like to start by running the vision by the VP of Marketing. Three team members and Mia decided to present the vision to the VP and share the process of how they arrived at the statement.

Sometimes, teams want to keep the vision to themselves, feeling a sense of ownership and camaraderie, like a private club. That's perfectly okay if the vision serves its purpose. If teams choose to share it, they need a plan for how and with whom it is shared. Getting the team involved in the communication, as in Mia's approach, gets further buy-in and increased commitment.

Cultivate

This is the final step of the process. A vision isn't worth anything if, once drafted, linked, and tested, it isn't implemented. As the old saying goes, "Off the walls and into the halls." That's the whole point, and the reason we go through all of this effort. The cultivation step is about building mechanisms into the daily work that bring forward the vision when decision-making, prioritizing, influencing, creating goals, and more. In other words, cultivation means making the vision and what it stands for a focal point of the team's work.

The Cultivate phase is owned by the leader. Mia strategically wove the vision into her team's daily work. Whether in one-on-ones or team meetings, decisions and debates were filtered through questions like: "Will this create brand loyalty?" or "Is this an example of us being a creative engine?" Eventually, the team normalized this behavior and began to do it on their own without Mia's prompting.

Cultivating requires discipline and tenacity, but when done well, it creates alignment and accountability and brings meaning to the team's work.

A compelling vision ignites motivation because employees know what they're working toward and why it is important. This builds commitment and focus and creates a bond among team members. Integrating a vision into the team's daily practices, processes, and behaviors can initially feel overwhelming and may lead to resistance and discomfort. However, persisting through these initial challenges leads to the vision becoming a guiding principle in day-to-day operations and a natural part of your team's ethos.

DEFINE THE VISION SUMMARY

Understanding the "why," "when," and "how" of envisioning are key to implementing a statement that will empower your team and ensure everyone is headed in the right direction.

Why a Vision?

Defining and cultivating a vision is a powerful way to bring clarity and direction to a team. As the opening quote stated, a team without direction may move, but it won't reach its destination.

Purpose of a vision:

- **Creates focus:** Provides a clear direction and purpose, helping team members understand what they are working toward.
- **Builds alignment:** Ensures that all team members are on the same page, working toward common goals and priorities.
- **Motivates the team:** Inspires and energizes team members by giving their work meaning and showing them how their efforts contribute to the bigger picture.
- **Supports decision-making:** Acts as a filter for making decisions, ensuring that all actions are aligned with the team's goals.
- **Fosters a sense of belonging:** Creates a shared purpose that binds the team together, enhancing collaboration and cohesion.
- **Drives commitment:** Engages team members by making them feel invested in the team's success and the realization of its vision.
- **Facilitates communication:** Provides a common language and framework for discussing goals, progress, and challenges.

- **Encourages innovation:** By setting a clear destination, it allows team members to think creatively about how to achieve it, fostering a culture of innovation.

When to Define or Redefine?

Consider defining or redefining the vision when you observe the following indicators:

- A new team forms.
- Team members are unclear about their purpose or priorities.
- The team's activities are not clearly aligned with the broader organizational strategy.
- The team members are not engaged or feel stressed.
- The team experiences frequent conflicts or miscommunications.
- The business or competitive environment has changed significantly.
- There are new competitors with different business models.
- The organization has shifted its direction or strategy.
- The current vision no longer motivates or inspires the team.
- The vision is not being used to guide priorities and decision-making.
- The team's mandate or composition has changed.
- The team is experiencing issues like slow decision-making, low energy, silos, or ineffective collaboration.

How to Craft?

Following the Four Cs—create, connect, communicate, cultivate—ensures that the vision is not just a statement but a living guide that drives the team's actions and decisions every day.

- **Create:** Engage the team in brainstorming to gather input, reflect on the purpose, and draft a vision statement.
- **Connect:** Ensure the draft vision aligns with the broader organizational strategy and culture, creating a coherent direction.
- **Communicate:** Decide whether to keep the vision within the team or share it more broadly. If the latter, test the vision with key stakeholders to ensure clarity and gather buy-in.
- **Cultivate:** Integrate the vision into daily practices and decision-making processes. Reinforce its principles consistently until it becomes a natural part of the team's operations.

YOUR CHALLENGE

Having read this chapter, your challenge is to assess whether your team has a vision that is defined and clear for each team member. If you do not have a vision—create one. This can be done collaboratively or by you, the leader, but ensure there is buy-in with tons of communication and debate.

If you have a vision, examine how it serves the team. Is it woven throughout your discussions and considered when making decisions? If not, revisit the vision; maybe it needs tweaking or rebirthing. Perhaps it needs a shorter- or longer-term view. Has the company's strategy shifted, changing team priorities? Communicate the vision and discuss how it might serve your people to find greater meaning in their work, crystallize priorities, decrease stress, and build a stronger team dynamic.

When your employees can articulate a vision and strategy that's relevant to them and they truly care about its importance, you're one step closer to a team that reaches its full potential. Just watch the magic happen!

Chapter Four

SET EXPECTATIONS

"The quality of our expectations determines the quality of our action."
—ANDRÉ GODIN

Here's a statistic that may surprise you: 87 percent of employees say they would be more productive and would add greater value to the organization if they had clear expectations from their manager.

Imagine the impact—nearly nine out of ten employees believe that clarity from their leader is the key to unlocking their full potential and driving the organization forward. This percentage has steadily increased since we began to collect the data, a reflection of the modern fast-paced, hybrid workplace.

I know this number seems high, but think about it in terms of your own role—how would you benefit if you were clearer on what your manager expects from you? What would be different? How would you feel? Would it increase your productivity through sharper focus, reduce stress, or help you be a better leader? Godin's assertion that our actions are directly influenced by the clarity of our expectations holds true not just in theory but in our daily work lives.

Since becoming a leader, do you ever feel like you've been handed the controls to a sophisticated piece of machinery with the potential to achieve incredible results—yet you've been given no instructions? Each button and lever seems to promise success, but without clarity you are left to trial and error. Your intention is to reach your goals to master the controls, but the lack of guidance leaves you confused, burning through your fuel, and exhausted. This frustration can't be chalked up to a lack of ambition or ability but to flying blind due to the absence of clear expectations.

When we reflect on the 87 percent statistic from our own perspective as leaders, it seems more likely to be true.

How about your direct reports? Would you say that they are clear about what is expected of them and how you expect them to get things done? In this chapter, we'll discuss the importance of setting expectations and the art of doing so in a way that resonates with and empowers your people.

SETTING THE STAGE FOR PERFORMANCE

How important is setting expectations? It's the first of three fundamental elements in a cycle of performance enablement—a process that drives continuous growth and improvement and allows a team to move from strategy to action, and from action to results.

The performance enablement cycle:

Expectations: Define what successful performance looks like.

Feedback: Provide continuous feedback against those expectations.

Development: Build and refine people's skills for current and future roles.

Let's see how these three play together. The leader sets expectations, clearly articulating job responsibilities, priorities, how success will be measured, and the behaviors required to succeed. For instance, these expectations could be delivered by saying, "Your priority in the next six months is to improve client relations scores by ten percent. We have a lot of customer feedback in different parts of the organization that can be very useful for you to analyze. As a first step, it will be helpful if you gather information by reaching out to your colleagues in other departments and learning what data they possess. How do you feel about that? When would be a good time for us to touch base on your progress?"

After an expectation is agreed upon, the leader observes performance based on what was set. If the employee is meeting expectations, the leader provides specific positive feedback to reinforce the behavior. If performance is on track and there is confidence in the employee's abilities, the leader looks for development opportunities by providing stretch assignments that expose the direct report to new skills or knowledge. For example, if an employee shows potential in leadership, you might assign a small project to lead. Or you might challenge them to do things differently, for example, "You are doing really well at this task. Are there ways you can improve the efficiency of how you accomplish it?"

What if the new employee isn't meeting expectations, or there's a gap between expectations and performance? This is when a leader provides constructive feedback and identifies the root cause of the performance issue. From there, in partnership with the direct report, the leader creates a development plan to close the gaps.

These three elements of performance enablement are a continuous cycle that loops back to expectations every time new responsibilities are added, job requirements change, new priorities surface, or the direction changes. That process always starts with expectations—not feedback or development. Skipping over expectation-setting and jumping straight into feedback can lead to unintended consequences, as we'll discuss next.

EXPECTATIONS BEFORE FEEDBACK

When leaders realize an employee's performance is not where it needs to be, their instinct is often to provide feedback. While this is well-intentioned, starting with feedback can create feelings of being unfairly judged. Instead of building motivation, this approach can foster resentment, as the employee feels constantly corrected without understanding how to hit the mark. That's why it's critical to ensure expectations are clearly defined first, creating a solid foundation that feedback can reinforce.

When performance is off, ask yourself whether you have clearly communicated what you expect. If not, that's where you start. If yes, then you need to provide meaningful feedback and development—a process we'll discuss further in Chapter Eight.

Take, for example, the situation where a seasoned sales director—whom I was coaching at the time—mentored a new business development representative (BDR) with extensive sales experience in a different sector. There were essentially three aspects to the BDR's role: prospecting, booking demos, and closing new business. This BDR excelled at scheduling software demos with existing leads but struggled with prospecting. Given the BDR's short tenure, the manager was less concerned with closing sales and more with acquiring prospects. The director became concerned when it was evident that the sales funnel had started to dry up.

During one of our coaching sessions, the director asked

me for recommendations on how to provide feedback to the new employee. He wanted to be sensitive—not to demotivate the eager BDR—but the situation needed to be imminently addressed.

I asked if the BDR had the skills necessary to cold call. According to the sales director, the BDR had experience in prospecting. That led to another question: "Did the BDR know prospecting was an important part of the job?" The director said, "Of course! Every sales rep knows the importance of building up the funnel."

This sounded like a big assumption. I asked if the director ever had an explicit conversation about the importance of prospecting. The answer was no. As a result, the BDR, while capable, did not prioritize prospecting, instead allocating most of their time to booking demos.

Maybe the BDR was trying to prove themselves quickly and thought showing the number of demos would get a better reaction from the leader or the team than saying, "I've cold-called twenty-five prospects." Or perhaps booking demos seemed to be a faster path to meeting the revenue quota.

This is a prime example where the leader needed to have an expectations-setting conversation, not one that provided feedback. The BDR knew their job involved prospecting, but their idea of how much prospecting they should do did not match the leader's. The director needed to spell out how much time the BDR should be spending on each of their job responsibilities. Given the current situation, the director thought the best equation would be 30 percent of time spent on prospecting, 50 percent on booking demos, and 20 percent on closing. Later, as the funnel filled and the BDR built relationships with their clients, the ideal allocation would be 10 percent on prospecting, 60 percent on demos, and 30 percent on closing new business.

So, that was it! That's what the director of sales needed to be clear about. He needed to specifically state the importance of prospecting and how much time was needed in each area, linking it to the bigger picture of meeting revenue targets.

Once the director of sales had the expectation-setting conversation, the BDR's performance shifted drastically. The sales funnel began to fill up, and their confidence grew as they saw how prospecting contributed to the larger goals.

SETTING EXPECTATIONS BEYOND TASKS

The director of sales set expectations around the BDR's job responsibilities, which is key. But expectation-setting involves more than just outlining what needs to be done. It also requires paying attention to how things are done. While *task expectations* focus on specific goals, such as completing deliverables on time, or meeting performance targets, *behavioral expectations* shape the team culture and guide how employees need to act and interact within the workplace, and live the company's values.

Behavioral norms affect the environment in which tasks are completed. It's not just about meeting deadlines—it's also about how employees treat one another, how they engage in discussions, and how they embody the company's values in their day-to-day actions.

Setting clear behavioral expectations can transform how teams operate and collaborate. Wade Foster, co-founder and CEO of Zapier, set a company-wide expectation known as "plus one." Each day, employees are encouraged to contribute one extra thing that improves the company, process, or product, even in small ways. This simple but effective expectation builds a culture of continuous improvement and reinforces the importance of persistence in driving the company forward.

Together, task and behavioral expectations create a clear foundation that empowers individuals to not only meet their objectives but do so in a way that aligns with the broader vision and values of the team and organization.

Let's explore this balance.

When task expectations are needed:

Lolita is a team player who is positive and liked by the team. She brings a great energy and passion to everything she touches. She likes collaboration, and shows empathy toward her colleagues. However, Lolita struggles with meeting her project deadlines and has missed key milestones on several occasions. She's not clear on her specific priorities and often spends time on tasks that aren't directly aligned with the team's goals.

Analysis: In this scenario, Lolita excels at the behavioral aspects of her role, but without clear task expectations, her performance suffers. She lacks direction and focus, which impacts her ability to contribute effectively to the team's objectives. Providing task clarity would allow Lolita to channel her positive behaviors toward the right outcomes.

When behavioral expectations are needed:

Peter is a results-oriented account manager who consistently meets his sales targets. However, he tends to operate independently, often missing team meetings and failing to keep colleagues informed. His "lone wolf" approach is causing friction within the team, as they struggle to stay updated on key information that impacts shared projects.

Analysis: In this scenario, Peter excels at achieving his individual goals but lacks the behavioral alignment required for effective teamwork. While his results are valuable, his lack of communication and collaboration is hurting the team's cohesion. Setting clear expectations around his participation in team meetings and information-sharing will help Peter contribute to the overall success of the team, ensuring his results don't come at the expense of others.

Task and behavioral expectations are the yin and yang of performance. *Tasks* represent the structure—the focus on what needs to get done. *Behavioral*, on the other hand, brings in the flow—the way people work together to achieve those tasks. Like yin and yang, they are interconnected and cannot exist without each other. A team can hit every deadline but crumble without the right behaviors, just as harmonious teamwork can fall short without clear goals. Together, they create the balance that drives sustainable success.

CHALLENGES OF SETTING EXPECTATIONS

Think back to a recent project you delegated to someone. Were you satisfied with how the project was managed? Did it meet the desired outcomes? Did it achieve its full potential?

Whether your answer is yes or no, consider the following questions:

- Did you clearly communicate the desired outcomes?
- Did you discuss how best to execute the project?
- Did you collaborate about what good, excellent, and subpar outcomes look like?
- Did you have regular check-ins to provide feedback and reset expectations if needed? If yes, what do you think your

direct report would say? Would they echo your assessment? If no, why not? What held you back?

If you're like most leaders, these questions will probably cause you to realize there are some gaps and opportunities in setting your employees up for success.

Remember the 87 percent of people who said they would benefit from clearer expectations? To make things more interesting, in the same research, managers were asked if they spend time setting expectations with their direct reports. And 82 percent said yes! This is an interesting contradiction. Why do so many employees feel like they lack expectations while most leaders believe they are making things clear? Something isn't adding up.

During workshops with leaders, I explore with managers why this gap exists. Here is what comes up:

- **Assumed awareness:** Managers assume employees inherently know what is expected of them without explicit communication.
- **Relying on job descriptions:** Many leaders believe job descriptions provide enough clarity, overlooking the need for ongoing discussions.
- **Fear of micromanaging:** Some leaders worry that detailed conversations about expectations might come across as patronizing or controlling.
- **Unclear standards:** In some cases, the expectations themselves aren't well-defined, making it hard to communicate them effectively.
- **Time constraints:** Many leaders believe there isn't enough time to get into the nitty-gritty, leaving employees to figure things out on their own.

- **Concerns about pushback:** Leaders might avoid setting clear expectations due to the fear of receiving difficult questions or resistance.
- **Frequent goal shifts:** Constantly changing priorities can make it challenging to set and maintain clear expectations.

These are legitimate reasons for sure, but here's the deal: if you want to create a culture of high performance, optimum engagement, and transformative innovation, you must work with and around those challenges. Having an expectation-setting conversation can be difficult—maybe more difficult than giving constructive feedback—but perhaps that can serve as a reminder of why these discussions are so important and make such a huge difference.

SIGNS YOUR TEAM NEEDS CLARITY

If your team members are performing well despite unclear expectations, consider it a temporary win. Sustainable success requires an understanding of expectations and well-defined outcomes.

Here is how you can diagnose whether this Function needs attention:

- *Decreased productivity:* Employees may waste time on non-priority tasks or become paralyzed by uncertainty, not knowing which tasks to tackle first.
- *Poor quality of work:* Without clear guidelines, the quality of work can suffer as employees may not understand the standards or benchmarks they should be meeting.
- *Low morale:* Ambiguity can lead to frustration and dissatisfaction, which can, in turn, diminish employee morale and engagement.

- *Increased stress:* Employees may experience heightened stress due to the ambiguity of their roles and responsibilities, leading to burnout and mental fatigue.
- *Inefficient communication:* Teams may struggle with communication as they lack a clear understanding of what information needs to be shared, with whom, and when.
- *Poor relationships:* Without clear behavioral expectations, individual priorities could compete and impact relationships and collaboration.
- *Inability to measure performance:* Evaluating employee performance becomes challenging if expectations are not defined, which can lead to poor performance management and hinder professional growth.
- *Slow to change:* People resist change when they don't know what the change means to them.

If you notice any of these on your team, consider it your call to action. Situational awareness, right?

USING ORGANIZATIONAL VALUES TO SHAPE EXPECTATIONS

If your company has well-defined values, they can be a powerful tool for setting expectations, especially behavioral ones. When expectations are linked to the values, you create alignment between how your team executes their work and the organizational culture, giving greater meaning and a clearer rationale for why change is necessary. This also fosters a stronger connection to the organization's mission.

Let's look at Priya's example.

Priya, a manager in the finance department, had a highly capable team responsible for handling the company's financial reporting and forecasting. However, recently, she noticed growing tension while the team was completing their work. Meetings had become contentious, with some team members disengaging while others dominated discussions. The issue wasn't with their skills or knowledge but with unclear expectations around behavior and collaboration.

The company had a core value of Teamwork, which emphasized collaboration and respect. Priya realized using the value could help ground what she wanted to achieve.

She brought the team together for a candid discussion. She began by explaining that their work was strong, but they were not living up to the company's Teamwork value. She facilitated a conversation where team members shared their frustrations, and she actively listened to each perspective. Some were concerned about the aggressive push to meet deadlines, while others felt that collaboration was slowing them down.

Priya then guided the team in redefining what effective teamwork should look like in practice. They identified key behaviors that would embody the value of Teamwork, such as:

- Actively listening and allowing each person to contribute in meetings
- Communicating clearly about deadlines and ensuring accountability by regularly checking in on progress
- Seeking input from others before making decisions that impact the whole team

Once they agreed on these behaviors, Priya initiated specific tactics to reflect the Teamwork value in the team's regular activities:

- Daily fifteen-minute check-ins where each team member

provided an update on their progress, ensuring that everyone was aligned and had the opportunity to ask for support or input

- Shared digital project tracker, Asana, where priorities, deadlines, progress updates, and task assignments were visible to all
- Monthly meetings specifically dedicated to brainstorming and idea-sharing, where team members could present their challenges and offer solutions, fostering an environment of mutual support and problem-solving

This made the abstract value of Teamwork more actionable and relevant to their day-to-day responsibilities.

By leveraging the organizational Teamwork value, Priya was able to reset expectations in a meaningful way that aligned with the company's goals and led to improved harmony, better collaboration, and more consistent results. Organizational values can be a valuable tool for leaders because they serve as a guidepost for setting clear and consistent expectations, ensuring that both tasks and behaviors support the broader vision.

THE ART OF SETTING CLEAR EXPECTATIONS

Effective expectation-setting requires a dual focus: what task needs to be accomplished (e.g., hitting project milestones or completing software debugging by the end of a sprint) and the manner of its execution (e.g., collaboration, taking initiative, flexibility, and communication). If you're like most managers, discussing the "what" is the easier part—it's more tangible and measurable. The pitfall can be how much detail to provide so you are thorough enough but not perceived to be a micromanager. The real challenge, however, is discussing the "how" or the ambiguities around behavior. These are often more subjective and harder to quantify.

The following steps and suggestions will help you set clear, motivating tasks and behavioral expectations.

WORK THROUGH THE STEPS

Okay, time to get practical. Think of someone on your team whose performance is falling short in a specific area. Maybe it's someone you have already given feedback to or someone who is a superstar, but there is an element of their performance that needs tweaking. Now run this scenario through the expectation-setting process:

1. Crystallize What You Expect

Think about what you want. What would an ideal performance look like? What is the gap? What would help the employee focus on the right priorities and unblock their performance?

If you find that the expectation is difficult to crystallize, keep working at it by asking yourself those questions. If you don't know clearly what the expectations are for your direct reports or team, rest assured they won't either. Before going into the conversation, ensure your own clarity.

I once worked with someone who was exceptional at execution. I could count on him to get the work done to my exact standards, but he would not take initiative. And although the output was great, I needed him to make decisions and initiate tasks without discussing them with me first. I trusted him and knew he was capable. After working together for some time, I knew he was ready.

Before I talked to him, I crystallized the expectations in my mind. I wanted him to take more initiative in certain aspects of his job, which included taking over repetitive requests from clients, managing assessment administration, and managing workshop scheduling.

2. Confirm Their Perspective

Now that you know what the expectation is, ask yourself if the employee is aware. Have you explicitly discussed this expectation? Is it part of the job description?

If yes, and you are 100 percent sure—no assumptions—then you likely need to have a feedback conversation, which we will explore later in the book.

If not, then prepare for the expectation-setting conversation.

In my example, I initially did not have a conversation about taking greater initiative because I wrongly assumed that the employee would naturally want to take on greater responsibility and make more decisions. Why did I assume that? Because that's what I would do. I am also a bit of a control freak and like to call the shots. I've learned through personality assessments, however, that people are different—we all think and behave differently.

Instead of assuming or judging—why is the person doing or not doing something—simply have the conversation and ask the right questions to better understand their perspective and redirect as needed.

3. Decide When to Have the Conversation

Expectation-setting conversations can happen in real time, meaning when the issue comes up and you have time at the moment to discuss it. But given the hybrid world we live in, these conversations often happen during one-on-ones or after retrospectives or postmortems.

Finding the perfect time is not as important as having enough time to get into the right level of detail and dialogue. Even though the manager takes the lead in expectation-setting conversations, it is a collaborative process that might involve negotiation and debate. It's critical to carve out sufficient space and time for an in-depth, two-way conversation where both parties can explore the expectations, ask questions, and ensure full understanding.

4. Plan Your Entry Point

In my work with leaders, I find that one thing that trips them up is how to start the conversation. Finding a point of entry that puts the employee at ease and doesn't imply they aren't doing their job can be challenging.

Here are my go-to conversation starters:

- "Since this is a new role for you, I would like to spend some time talking through what the expectations are and how we can measure success."
- "I want to make sure we set you up for success. Let's review some key aspects of your role and ensure we are on the same page regarding expectations."
- "How do you see your role changing from the way you work now?"
- "What do you think will be the biggest challenge you will face in your role?"
- "Sometimes I rush through details, but I want to make sure that we have a good discussion about your job and expectations."

- "Our team's success relies on each of us understanding our roles deeply. Let's discuss what success in your role looks like and how it aligns with our team's goals."
- "Are there any areas of your work that are unclear or fuzzy?"

You know your people and yourself. Plan how you will start the conversation in a way that makes sense to the employee and feels authentic for you.

5. Get Buy-In

Buy-in means getting people on board—convincing them of the importance of the expectation. Be prepared to share reasons for why it's important for them. "It's your job" may not be motivating enough!

True buy-in isn't just about compliance—it's about commitment. It is through conversations where you create the understanding, connection, and relevance, helping your direct reports see how meeting the expectation not only contributes to the larger team goals but also to their personal growth and success.

Using the previous example of the BDR, the conversation to get buy-in might go like this:

Sales director: I want to set you up for success and ensure you're fully equipped to meet your targets. Building a solid sales pipeline is a big part of your success. By dedicating a set portion of your time to prospecting, you're not only laying the groundwork for your success but, by extension, the success of our team. I'm committed to supporting you in this. How much time do you think you need to allocate for prospecting?

BDR: I think about 5 to 10 percent, so I can focus on closing business and booking demos.

Sales director: I appreciate your focus on generating revenue quickly. That's a good mindset in sales. However, to achieve your revenue targets, a strong prospecting funnel is required. If you only spend 5 percent of your time prospecting, you risk not having enough qualified leads to sustain and grow the pipeline.

Our analytics show that to meet your targets and ensure consistent revenue, you need to dedicate about a third of your time to prospecting.

BDR: Wow, that's a lot.

Sales director: I know it might seem like that, but by increasing your prospecting efforts, you're actually setting the stage for quicker, more sustainable revenue growth. This will make booking demos and closing business smoother and more efficient because you will have a steady stream of potential clients to engage with.

How do you feel about gradually increasing your time prospecting? We could start with, say, 20 percent this week and then aim for a third over the next few weeks. I am here to help you with any challenges that come up as you make this shift.

BDR: Okay, let me try that this week.

Sales director: Just remember the point of increasing prospecting is to have a healthy pipeline. Once you achieve that, it will be up to you to monitor and adjust the time you spend on it.

BDR: Thanks for the guidance. I will keep you updated.

Sales director: Perfect, let's touch base next week to see how it's going and if you need anything.

This conversation illustrates how setting expectations goes beyond simply stating requirements—it's about ensuring that the employee understands the rationale behind them and feels supported in reaching their goals. By engaging in a dialogue and addressing concerns, the sales director not only gained buy-in but also built a foundation of trust and collaboration. The employee left the conversation with a clear plan and the confidence that they had support along the way.

6. Agree on Documentation and Follow-Up

Some expectations are simple and may not need to be documented or followed up on. For example, if you both agree that a month-end report will be completed by the second day of each month, you might not need to follow up unless the employee continues to struggle with meeting the expectation.

However, when expectations are critical to the job and the employee's performance will be measured against them, documentation is essential. This is especially true for more complex or high-impact tasks.

Often-used frameworks include OKRs, KPIs, and SMART. There are others but keep it simple; no need to reinvent the wheel. It's less about the framework and more about clearly communicating expectations to your team, ensuring they understand what success and follow-up look like.

Let's explore these:

OKRs (Objectives and Key Results)

OKRs are best for setting overarching, ambitious, aspirational goals with a focus on learning and iteration. For example, if your objective is to improve system reliability, you might set key results such as:

1. Achieve a system uptime of 99.9 percent over the next quarter.
2. Decrease the mean time to resolve (MTTR) critical incidents by 50 percent within two months.
3. Implement a disaster recovery plan by year's end.

KPIs (Key Performance Indicators)

KPIs are best for tracking steady, incremental improvements with precise, measurable metrics. For the same system reliability objective, KPIs might include:

1. Monthly system uptime of 99.9 percent with less than thirty minutes of unplanned downtime.
2. A 50 percent reduction in MTTR for critical incidents over two months.
3. Full implementation of a disaster recovery plan by year-end, measured against a checklist.

Notice how these KPIs mirror the key results of the OKR example, but with a focus on measurable, ongoing performance.

SMART Goals

SMART goals combine the flexibility of OKRs with the precision of KPIs, ensuring goals are specific, measurable, achievable, relevant, and time-bound.

For example, "Within the next twelve months, reduce system downtime and improve incident resolution times to enhance system reliability" is a SMART goal because it clearly defines what needs to be achieved, how progress will be measured, and sets a specific deadline.

All three frameworks are effective tools for setting and communicating expectations. The key is to choose the one that best fits your team's needs and the nature of the goals you're setting, making certain that everyone understands what success looks like.

Some of you may be wondering what to do if you go through these steps and behavior doesn't change. Hang on; we'll get to that in Chapter Eight. For now, let me say that if you observe behaviors that are not aligned with the culture of the team, you must address them. Don't wait in hopes that it will go away. What we don't stop, we promote.

TAILOR EXPECTATIONS TO PERSONALITY PREFERENCES

Working through the above steps provides you with techniques to overcome the challenges of setting expectations. However, personalizing these conversations allows you to address individual preferences and motivations, creating an environment where clarity is enhanced and buy-in naturally follows.

For example, maybe you have a team member who lives and breathes data. They dive deep into analysis, always needing one more piece of information before making a decision. While their detail-oriented approach is invaluable, you notice that it sometimes slows down the process more than necessary, creating a bottleneck when speed is of the essence. You could tailor your expectations to their preference for detail by clarifying time constraints and setting specific parameters for how much data is needed. For example, you might say, "I know your attention to detail is a huge asset, and I want to balance that with the need to move quickly. Let's set a limit on the amount of research time—after three data points, let's move forward with a decision."

By framing the expectation in a way that acknowledges their strengths while guiding them toward a more balanced approach, you create clarity and increase the likelihood of buy-in, as the conversation respects their working style.

Tools like Everything DiSC can be incredibly helpful in understanding and speaking to these preferences. They give you insight into what employees deem important, where they spend their time, and what motivates them, all of which can guide your expectation-setting conversations.

Most personality assessments, including DiSC, are based on two key dimensions: task-oriented versus people-oriented and fast-paced versus moderate-paced. When these dimensions cross over, they create four distinct clusters of behaviors, each representing a different approach to work and communication:

1. **Dominance (D):** Task-oriented and fast-paced, these individuals are direct, assertive, and driven by results.
2. **Influence (i):** Motivated by relationships, creativity, and recognition, these individuals are people-oriented, fast-paced, enthusiastic, and social.
3. **Steadiness (S):** People-oriented and moderate-paced, these individuals are patient and supportive and have a preference for stability and harmony.

4. **Conscientiousness (C):** Task-oriented and moderate-paced, these individuals are detail-focused, analytical, and motivated by accuracy and precision.

Each style has unique strengths and blind spots. By understanding these styles, leaders can anticipate potential roadblocks to performance and set more effective expectations that better set their team members up for success.

Let's look at some examples, including what you might say and your focus as a leader.

Dominance (D): Employees who are driven, results-oriented, like to make quick decisions, and often take charge of situations tend to have a D style, representing Dominance. These individuals are often seen as direct, assertive, and pioneering. However, they might assume that speed and decisiveness are always the top priorities, potentially overlooking the value of collaboration or detailed planning.

When setting expectations, set high but achievable goals that push them to stretch their abilities. Challenges stimulate their drive for results and keep them engaged. While D styles are great at driving projects forward, emphasize the importance of team input and diverse perspectives, encouraging them to seek and value the contributions of others.

What you might say: "Sam, I know you're focused on moving this project forward. Let's also make sure we're incorporating feedback from the team so you have the information to make quick decisions. I'd like you to lead the next meeting, but take some time to gather input from everyone first—it will help ensure we're all aligned and moving in the right direction."

Focus: Balance their drive for results with the need for collaboration.

Influence (i): When I worked for Hilton Hotels, I had a

team member who was the life of the office. She had a lot of ideas and loved to communicate and collaborate. She is an example of an i or Influence style, thriving in social, collaborative, and dynamic team environments.

I once asked her to do research for a specific project I was working on. She did an amazing job, but the information came to me as a mixed salad of different documents in different locations. There was no cohesion or order to the madness. I wanted to receive succinctly presented information with pre-drawn conclusions.

While i style individuals are great at generating excitement, they might overlook details or fail to follow through on tasks as new, more exciting ideas come up. It's important to be clear about the outcomes you expect and the steps needed to get there. Use their preference for verbal communication to discuss these expectations openly, ensuring they understand the importance of structure and follow-through.

What you might say: "Jessie, your creativity is what we need for this project. How about you pull together the key ideas into one document with your recommendations and timelines? We can chat about it before you dive into the next phase."

Focus: Balance their idea generation and enthusiasm with follow through.

Steadiness (S): Do you have a team member who is reliable, supportive, and genuinely concerned with maintaining harmony within the team? They tend to be quiet as they try to read the situation or give space for others to contribute. This person likely embodies the S style in the DiSC® model, representing Steadiness.

Individuals with an S style personality are known for their calm demeanor, cooperative nature, and preference for stable, predictable environments. They might assume that their primary role is to maintain the status quo, potentially hesitating to suggest changes or take initiative. These employees need to be reassured that taking the initiative on new ideas or challenging the status quo is necessary and that they will be supported throughout the transition.

What you might say: "Taylor, I really appreciate how you bring a calm and steady presence to the team, especially with all the changes we're going through. I'd love to get your take on how we can make this process even better. The team has been struggling with it, and I think you making some adjustments to it could really help ease some of the stress. I know this would mean another change, but it's important for everyone's well-being in the long run. How about you suggest some tweaks, and then we can discuss how you can help guide the team through the transition? I'll be right there with you to make sure everyone understands why this change is necessary."

Focus: Balance their need for stability with the need for change.

Conscientiousness (C): Our data-loving team member from the earlier example likely leans towards the C or Conscientiousness style, characterized by accuracy, attention to detail, and independence. Such employees might assume that perfection is the expectation, driving them to overanalyze and polish their work before moving forward.

As a leader, it's important to set clear, specific goals that guide how much time should be spent on analysis. Discuss and establish an endpoint for the employee's research, helping to curb the tendency to overanalyze. Determine when 80 percent effort is enough to avoid unnecessary delays.

What you might say: "Zilia, your attention to detail is awesome, and I always appreciate it. For this project, we don't need a full dive into the data; high-level information will be enough.

Let's aim to have the analysis done by Wednesday. We can review it together then and see if anything else should be added."

Focus: Balance their need to get things right with efficiency.

When we tailor expectations to someone's personality, it's like playing their favorite song. Even in the most crowded space they hear it, appreciate it, and immediately tune in. By speaking in a way that matches their preferences, we not only capture their attention but also encourage genuine engagement and commitment.

RECOGNIZING THE DISC STYLES

Identifying the DiSC styles of your team members doesn't require a formal assessment right away. Start by observing behaviors and communication patterns.

Here's a quick guide to help you spot the different styles:

Dominance (D): Task-oriented and fast-paced, these individuals are direct, assertive, and driven by results.

- *Look for:* Fast decision-makers who get to the point, prioritize tasks, and often take charge.
- *Signs:* They are focused on results, enjoy challenges, and might appear impatient or blunt.

Influence (i): Motivated by relationships, creativity, and recognition, these individuals are people-oriented, fast-paced, enthusiastic, and social.

- *Look for:* Outgoing individuals who focus on opportunities, like to collaborate, and like being in the spotlight.
- *Signs:* They are often seen as talkative, persuasive, and enjoy engaging others in discussions.

Steadiness (S): People-oriented and moderate-paced, these individuals are patient and supportive and have a preference for stability and harmony.

- *Look for:* Calm, reliable team members who value structure and a conflict-free environment.
- *Signs:* They tend to be on the quiet side, prefer a steady pace, and are supportive of others.

Conscientiousness (C): Task-oriented and moderate-paced, these individuals are detail-focused, analytical, and motivated by accuracy and precision.

- *Look for:* Steady individuals who focus on quality, like to be seen as experts, and prefer a systematic approach.
- *Signs:* They often focus on accuracy, prefer clear guidelines, and might be cautious before making decisions.

In addition, pay attention to how your team members react under stress or when facing deadlines. Under pressure the styles come out more, highlighting natural tendencies, and can provide further clues to their DiSC style.

Each team member, with their distinct work style and preferences, contributes to the rich diversity that can drive your team toward unparalleled success. There is no better or worse style. The key lies in understanding and harnessing these differences.

We will explore working styles later in the book, but for now, it's important to know that all personality styles are valuable, and each of us possesses traits from various styles. It's not a matter of being unable to do certain things but rather how we adapt or "flex" our natural tendencies to meet different needs.

If you would like to use the DiSC® assessment to learn more about yourself or your team, my company website can provide the information: www.fullcircleconnections.ca.

BE INTENTIONAL ABOUT PRIORITIES

One of the biggest pain points I see in the workplace is the constant buzz that everything is important and urgent. Setting clear priorities with your employees is an absolute must in leadership today. Intentional action is a leadership pillar that should be shared and emphasized at every level. It answers these questions: Why do I choose to do this instead of something else? How does this align with the bigger picture, the vision? Without clear priorities, teams lose focus and direction. As I mentioned earlier, if everything is important, nothing is important.

Leaders are often reluctant to provide that clarity for fear that other tasks won't get air time, but by establishing priorities, you're not pushing other tasks aside; rather, you're ensuring your team is laser-focused on what truly moves the needle. People are smart, and they will understand that other things need to be done, but they will also make smarter decisions about how they spend their time.

I made writing this book my priority. That didn't mean that I stopped delivering workshops and coaching for two years. It meant that I used my priority as a filter to make decisions. During the course of my writing, Patrick Lencioni launched a new program based on his book, *The 6 Types of Working Genius*. I got super excited about getting certified in the program so I could provide my clients with another tool. However, my first priority was this book. Investing time and money in Patrick's course would have taken me away from that priority. Now that the book is published, I can go back and revisit the certification.

Without a guiding hierarchy of tasks, vital projects can get lost in the daily hustle. When we don't know what our priorities are, we tend to fill our days with busywork. When the work we do aligns with our priorities, however, we get greater satisfaction and meaning from our efforts.

By setting and communicating clear priorities, you empower your team members to work smarter, reduce unnecessary stress, and keep everyone aligned with the most critical goals. In doing so, you establish a foundation of intentional action that drives your team toward success.

QUICK NOTE ON JOB DESCRIPTIONS

Job descriptions age like milk and not wine. They don't age well.

A quick hack for ensuring job clarity is to have an up-to-date job description. You can delegate this task to the employee. Ask them to review the description and add, delete, or edit based on the work they currently do. I find most employees like going through this process because it gives them a voice in defining what they do, provides clarity about what they do, and also makes them feel like what they do creates value.

Once they've made their revisions, take time for a meaningful discussion. This is a chance to dive deep into their perspective on their role and priorities, and how they match up with the team's goals. These conversations can significantly strengthen alignment, trust, and mutual understanding.

This approach to keeping job descriptions relevant not only ensures they stay up-to-date but also fosters a culture of ownership and transparency. It's a strategic yet straightforward way to navigate the ever-changing landscape.

WHEN YOU DON'T KNOW WHAT YOU DON'T KNOW

Let's be honest—there are times when you think, "What the hell am I supposed to expect here?" If you've ever found yourself in that boat, you're not alone. Here's the thing—when the road map isn't clear, co-navigate with your employee. Get them involved, and ask questions like: "How would you approach this situation?" "What do you think is key for us to focus on?" "By when do you think you will be able to complete this?" "What's missing in our report that could really amp it up?" and "How much of your week should we dedicate to this project to hit the milestone?"

In addition, get into the habit of asking, "Out of everything on your plate, what's the real game changer here? Why does it top your list?" Or bring your team together after an all-hands and ask questions like, "What do you think the shift in the strategy means to our team?" and "Do we need to shift our priorities?" This not only helps you see how your employees understand the expectations, but also empowers them to take ownership of their work.

You don't need to have all the answers. Your role as a leader is to leverage the intelligence of others and collaborate to find the best route to success.

JUST TELL THEM!

So many problems arise or get worse simply because we shy away from being direct with expectations. When I say "direct," I don't mean rude or pushy. We always want to be soft on the person, and hard on the issue. But sometimes we really make a bigger deal out of situations than they ought to be. We need to buckle up, breathe in some courage, and deal with issues up front.

What eventually balloons into a major issue could potentially be eliminated if we simply communicated directly.

Here are some typical complaints I hear from managers. If you are dealing with any of these, I have some questions for you to ask in response:

Manager: "They don't get back to me as agreed."
Me: "Have you openly discussed this expectation with them?"

Manager: "They're unprepared for meetings."
Me: "Did you clearly state the meeting prep you expected?"

Manager: "They don't contribute in meetings."
Me: "Have you encouraged them to share their thoughts?"

Manager: "They look frumpy and unprofessional."
Me: "Have you shared with them what 'professional' means in our context?"

Manager: "They're consistently late."

Me: "Have you explored the reasons why and set clear expectations?"

You get the idea, right? Just tell them! Yes, these conversations can be uncomfortable and difficult, but you are a leader and doing difficult things is part of the job. We will address difficult conversations later in the book, but buckle up—courage is a big trait of a successful leader.

BE THE ROLE MODEL

The final piece of the art of expectation-setting is to remember this crucial truth: You, as a leader, are the role model. Your actions set expectations.

Here's an interesting exercise: Examine your team's behaviors and reflect on how inadvertently your actions influence theirs. Ask yourself, "Did my actions today inspire the behavior I want to see in my team?" Recognize the discrepancies and act differently the next day. Walk the talk and embody the expectations you set for others. If you want accountability, deliver on your promises. If you want collaboration, don't dominate conversations. If you want honesty, show vulnerability. Set a good example of what you want to see.

Leadership comes with its set of dilemmas, like balancing vulnerability with authority. It's natural to fear that your leadership might be undermined if you strive for honesty and openness. However, finding a balance between genuine vulnerability and position can strengthen trust and encourage a more open, communicative team environment.

Remember: the most powerful expectation-setting tool is your own example.

SET EXPECTATIONS SUMMARY

Setting expectations is a fundamental leadership function that provides clarity, direction, and focus for your team, enabling them to prioritize efforts, make informed decisions, and take ownership of their work. However, leaders often rush past this task, assuming that expectations are obvious or already understood. This can lead to misalignment, frustration, and burnout.

Clear expectations, both in terms of tasks and behaviors, are essential to translating the organization's values into daily actions and fostering a high-performance culture. When communicated effectively, expectations create accountability, trust, and alignment with team and organizational goals, ultimately driving productivity and engagement. This chapter highlights the importance of not only setting expectations but doing so in a way that resonates with and empowers your people.

Why Setting Expectations Matters

Setting expectations is a cornerstone of effective leadership. Doing so:

- Increases productivity by providing clarity
- Reduces stress and uncertainty for employees
- Encourages accountability and alignment with team goals
- Enhances team morale and collaboration
- Fosters a culture of high performance and innovation

When to Set Expectations

These are some of the most common times when it becomes critical to make sure you've set clear expectations for your team members:

- Onboarding new employees or transitioning roles
- Introducing new tasks, projects, or priorities
- When there's a performance gap or behavior that needs addressing
- At the beginning of a project or initiative to ensure alignment
- When priorities shift, or organizational changes occur

How to Set Expectations

Setting expectations involves good communication. Plan your strategy. Here are some of the key areas that I suggest leaders take to heart:

- Focus on the "what" and the "how" of what you expect from your employees.
- Crystallize your desired outcome.
- Use tools like OKRs, KPIs, and SMART goals to ensure measurability.
- Plan how to start the conversation before you begin.
- Align expectations with the organizational values.
- Involve team members in the expectation-setting process to gain buy-in.
- Personalize what you want from your employees to individual work styles.
- Utilize the job description to create a positive feedback loop for what you expect.
- Regularly revisit and adjust expectations based on performance and changing priorities.
- Be a role model for your people and lead by example.

YOUR CHALLENGE

Now that you've explored the Set Expectations Function, it's time to put this knowledge into practice.

Step 1: Reflect on Your Current Approach

Take a moment to evaluate how clearly you're currently setting expectations with your team.

Ask yourself:

- How often do I articulate clear, specific expectations?
- Are my expectations aligned with both individual and organizational goals?
- How do I ensure that my team members understand what success looks like?

Step 2: Choose One Team Member

Identify one team member who could benefit from clearer expectations. This could be someone who is new to the role, someone who has struggled to meet expectations, or even a high performer ready for new challenges.

Step 3: Have an Expectations-Setting Conversation

Schedule a one-on-one meeting with this team member. Review the "Work Through the Steps" section of the chapter to prepare for and navigate the conversation.

Step 4: Implement a Feedback Loop

Set up a follow-up meeting to review progress. Discuss any challenges they've faced and adjust expectations if necessary.

Step 5: Reflect and Adjust

After your follow-up meeting, reflect on the process:

- Did the clarity of your expectations lead to better performance or engagement?

- How did the feedback loop contribute to their understanding and motivation?
- What would you do differently next time to improve your expectation-setting skills?

Step 6: Expand the Practice

Once you've completed this challenge with one team member, start applying the same process with others on your team. The goal is to make setting clear expectations a natural and consistent part of your leadership approach. By mastering the art of clear expectations, you're not only setting your team up for success but also strengthening your own ability to lead with clarity and purpose.

Be aware of the pitfalls described in this function. Don't fall prey to assumptions. Above all, come away from this chapter with a newfound reverence for expectations and the vital role they play. Now it's time to ignite that motivation within your people.

Chapter Five

IGNITE MOTIVATION

"People often say that motivation doesn't last. Well, neither does bathing—that's why we recommend it daily."

—ZIG ZIGLER

Motivation is an interesting concept. It comes and goes, makes us do things we didn't know we could, and sometimes disappears when we need it most. It's the burst of energy that gets us out of bed early for a morning run, or convinces us to hit snooze instead.

I experience this ebb and flow every time I restart my workout regime. I make a plan, schedule my gym time, maybe get some new Lulus, and for the first few days I am all in! But then something happens, a friend wants to meet up for a drink, I feel tired after a long day, or maybe my muscles feel sore. Suddenly that motivation is nowhere to be found.

At work, it's no different. The beginning of a project or initiative can energize, but as the weeks go by, keeping that momentum going can be a struggle. The daily grind itself can also wear you down—too much change, not enough change; too much collaboration, not enough collaboration. You get it!

When you're unmotivated, the smallest hill can look like a mountain. Challenges and obstacles that once seemed manageable can feel ridiculously hard, like climbing Mount Everest in flip-flops.

Have you ever felt like this? Like the weight of the climb is heavier than it used to be and you're no longer enthusiastic about charging up the hill? If so, you know that it takes real effort to regain the motivation that once kept you going.

Now, imagine you're not the one standing at the base of that hill—it's your employee. As leaders, we often focus on goals and outcomes, but it's just as important to remember that those results are achieved by people, some of whom might have lost motivation and are struggling with their own Mount Everests.

What can you do to help your team find their drive again? How can you support them in making that daily climb feel less daunting? That's what this chapter is all about. We'll explore the true nature of motivation and how to *ignite* the motivation that already exists within your employees. We'll also delve into strategies, tools, and insights that reignite motivation in your team, helping them feel empowered, energized, and ready to tackle the challenges of today.

IGNITING, NOT MOTIVATING

Let's bust a myth: none of us has the power to motivate anyone. What we can do is to ignite what already exists within a person. When I realized this subtle but important distinction, I had a big "aha moment" that changed my entire approach to leadership.

An old but appropriate story perfectly illustrates this concept: A fisherman sits on the dock casting his rod into a lake. A passerby asks, "Hey! How's the fishing?" The fisherman answers, "Nothing, not even a bite."

The passerby says, "That's odd, the lake is full of fish."

The fisherman adamantly replies, "Well, not today. They ain't biting."

The passerby then asks, "What are you using for bait?"

The fisherman pulls his reel out of the water and exposes the hook, which has a strawberry dangling from its barbed end. The confused passerby asks, "A strawberry?" To which the fisherman responds, "Doesn't everyone love strawberries?"

Leaders often make a similar assumption: that everyone is motivated by the same things they are.

But motivation isn't one-size-fits-all. Each person is driven by different factors—what ignites one person might not even spark interest in another. That's why it's crucial for leaders to take the time to truly understand what makes their team members tick.

This requires knowing our employees and understanding what they want, need, and desire and then moving toward that.

The bottom line is don't fish with strawberries. Get to know your people and ignite what already exists inside of them. When you align your leadership efforts with your employees' true motivators, you don't just inspire them—you empower them to achieve beyond what they thought possible.

But why is motivation so important? Why is it one of the Functions of a leader? There is a powerful connection between motivation and engagement. Let's explore engagement first.

MORE THAN A BUZZWORD

"Engagement" has become such a buzzword in organizations that I can see leaders reaching for their phones the moment I mention it because they've lost interest. Even though it often takes center stage, it remains obscure, unclear, and hard for many leaders to act on. Most companies conduct regular surveys to get the organizational pulse, and when results reveal a gap—a hint that all is not as it should be—the corporate engine starts churning. Traditionally, this involves meetings, action plans, and strategies designed to bridge the divide between existing disengagement and desired engagement.

And let's be honest—it can feel like a punch to the gut when the effort you've put in doesn't seem to show up in the numbers. If you've been in leadership for a while, you've likely been tasked with decoding your team's survey results and translating them into actionable insights. This process can feel very personal, not to mention demanding on your time and resources. Because the analysis is rarely linked to the bigger "why," creating an action plan often feels like a project that detracts from "real work." No wonder these surveys create skepticism and affect how engagement initiatives are perceived and prioritized.

Totally understandable! *But*—yes, there is a big *but* here—the results cannot be dismissed or treated like just another box to tick. In fact, they are a real gift, offering insights into how your direct reports feel. Poor results are a genuine opportunity to adjust and realign. Engagement is not a constant; it's something that evolves as we grow. A dip in engagement isn't necessarily a reflection of your abilities as a leader—sometimes, it's simply a part of the natural cycle of growth and evolution within a team.

Because engagement has become an overused buzzword, managers sometimes deprioritize or dismiss it altogether. If this sounds familiar, consider this: your team's level of engagement is significantly shaped by your actions. Gallup's research shows that 70 percent of employees' engagement is directly influenced by their manager. Yes, 70 percent!

This may be hard to digest, but reflect for a moment on

your own experiences. Have you ever decided to leave a job, not because of the job itself, but because of your manager? When you think of a time when you were particularly demotivated at work, how much would you say was due to the manager? Now think about your employees and your influence on how they feel.

Periods of disengagement are very stressful for the employee and frustrating for the manager. I have coached a few people for whom this type of disengagement lasted for most of their careers. Imagine!

We often think that when people disengage, they leave, but we've all heard of quiet quitting. A lot happens, or doesn't happen, during the period between disengagement and leaving. Employees may clock in, but their contributions are often limited and their enthusiasm fades. This quiet withdrawal can lead to productivity decreases, creativity stalls, missed opportunities, delayed projects, and a general decline in team morale.

Look, engagement is the engine of productivity; it's not a metric to be improved but a critical driver of organizational performance. By focusing on engagement, companies invest in their most valuable asset—their people—which in turn translates into improved productivity. Engaged teams bring more energy and passion to their work; they drive tangible results. Research consistently shows that when employees feel connected to their work, productivity soars. They're more likely to stick around, reducing turnover costs and contributing to a positive, dynamic work environment that fuels innovation and growth.

Bottom line: engagement is a key strategic priority for leaders looking to cultivate a high-performing team.

But here's the key: the path to true engagement is through motivation. To create a genuinely engaged team, you must understand what drives your people at their core. Engagement and motivation are deeply interconnected, each influencing the other in a dynamic interplay.

ENGAGEMENT AND MOTIVATION CONNECTION

Understanding the distinction between employee engagement and motivation can significantly enhance how you lead your team to achieve their full potential.

At its core, **engagement** is the emotional and psychological investment an individual has toward their work and their organization. It's about feeling connected with the bigger purpose, valued and secure—a sense of belonging, significance, and achievement within the workplace. **Motivation**, on the other hand, is the driving force that propels us toward goals and outcomes, fueled by our intrinsic desires and extrinsic rewards.

My personal key motivators, for example, include initiating change, achieving immediate results, innovating, and taking risks. When I am in an environment that allows for these to be at play at least some of the time, I see the work as meaningful and valuable, and my engagement levels rise, which reinforces the motivation to share my discretionary effort, take on new challenges, and strive for excellence.

But can there be engagement without motivation? Yes, it's possible. An employee might feel loyal and connected to the organization's mission or values but lack the drive to go above and beyond if their day-to-day tasks aren't stimulating. For instance, someone working at a nonprofit whose mission they deeply believe in might feel a strong sense of belonging (engagement) but could struggle to stay motivated if their role doesn't challenge them or offer growth opportunities. This could lead them to do their work without the extra effort that drives initiative, innovation, and excellence.

On the other hand, motivation without engagement is also possible. An individual might be highly motivated by personal goals, such as career advancement or financial rewards, but if they don't feel connected to the company's culture or values, they might not stick around long-term. They might excel in their role and deliver results (motivation) but could be disengaged with the company itself, making them more likely to leave for another opportunity that offers both engagement and motivation.

Ideally, you want both engagement and motivation in your team. While engagement provides a foundation of connection and belonging, motivation is the spark that fuels action, creativity, and excellence. This is why igniting motivation is so critical. When it is missing, engagement often declines. When motivation is present, however, it has the power to energize people so they choose to work harder, which leads to sustained individual and organizational success.

DISCRETIONARY EFFORT

The funny thing about that steep hill is that for engaged employees, it is challenging *and* exhilarating—a chance to push limits, innovate, and achieve. They are willing to take on the hill not because they have to but because they *want* to. That's discretionary effort—the difference between doing what is required and going above and beyond. This is what propels teams and organizations forward, turning ordinary outcomes into extraordinary achievements. When people find meaning in what they do, they have an abundance of energy they are happy to share.

What does discretionary effort look like? Well, for one, bigger questions are asked. Employees not only do the work they were hired to do, but also become observant about how the work is being done. They come up with different and more innovative ways to achieve desired results. They ask questions like: "Why do we have that process?" "Why do we need to do this?" "What do our stakeholders truly want?"

Employees willing to give discretionary effort aren't afraid to fail. They embrace the process—fail, iterate, repeat—always looking for better ways to succeed.

But discretionary effort doesn't happen by chance. It's a direct result of how motivated and engaged an individual feels.

For example, take a project I worked on with a client in the tech industry. They were launching a new software product, and the team had a tight deadline. One of the developers, Emma, was highly engaged with the project. She believed in the product's potential and felt personally connected to its goals. Without being asked, Emma stayed late several nights to refine the user interface, ensuring it was not just functional but also intuitive and visually appealing. Her discretionary effort didn't just help meet the deadline—it elevated the product's quality, making it a standout success with early users.

Emma's extra effort wasn't about working longer hours; it was about her willingness to go the extra mile because she found the work meaningful and knew her contributions were valued. This is the essence of discretionary effort—working smarter, finding better ways to achieve results, and taking initiative when it's needed most.

As a leader, your role is to create the conditions where discretionary effort thrives—where employees are motivated and empowered to take ownership of their work and encouraged to innovate. When they know their efforts make a difference, they'll keep giving that extra, even when things get tough. Every team member has unique reasons for going the extra mile—your job is to find what ignites that motivation and create an environment that fuels it.

But there's another key piece of the puzzle to consider: the link between effort and results. Motivation may spark the initial effort, but sustained engagement often depends on the outcomes people experience. Let's unpack how effort and results feed into one another and how, as a leader, you can ensure your team feels rewarded for their hard work.

THE EFFORT AND RESULTS EQUATION

There is a simple yet powerful equation to keep in mind when igniting motivation—the balance of effort versus results, particularly in how individuals respond to varying levels of effort and reward.

When effort produces tangible results, individuals are driven to keep putting in the work. This positive feedback loop reinforces engagement and performance.

Conversely, when minimal effort still yields results, individuals may feel content but stop doing extra, as the perceived need for sustained work diminishes. This can create a scenario where motivation is high initially but drops off as success comes too easily.

On the other hand, when individuals put in significant effort without seeing results, disengagement often follows. This pattern is supported by research on job burnout, where high effort without corresponding rewards can lead to emotional exhaustion and a subsequent decline in engagement.

Effort + Results = **Motivation**
Low Effort + Results = **Short-Term Motivation**
Effort + No Results = **Disengagement**

I am going to use an example that is near and dear to my heart: dieting!

When I go on a diet and really watch what I eat, stick to the plan, and see the type of results I want, I keep going! There's no stopping me.

When I go on a diet but cheat here and there with an occasional glass of wine, piece of chocolate, or dinner with friends and still—surprisingly—get the result I want, I am super happy, but I become less diligent as time goes on. Why not keep sneaking in those guilty pleasures? After all, it's working, right?

But when I really watch what I eat and exercise and the scale doesn't budge, frustration sets in. I get demotivated and eventually disengage altogether.

The reason why I share this with you is because sometimes, no matter how motivated someone is, if the effort doesn't produce the expected results, demotivation is inevitable and is usually followed by disengagement. The same holds true for your team. When setting expectations, giving feedback, or acknowledging performance, reinforce the connection between effort and results. Be explicit about what matters most; otherwise, the default assumption will always be that results are the priority. And although, ultimately, we want results, sometimes the effort is what matters because it can set the team up for bigger wins down the line, while easy gains can lead to complacency and a drop in motivation later.

> **Example of when effort is more important:** A new team member tasked with heading up a client proposal for the first time. Despite putting in long hours and thoroughly preparing, the client hasn't signed off yet. As the leader, you recognize the effort and highlight how attention to detail and a proactive approach have laid a strong foundation for future success. In this case, it's important

to reinforce the value of their effort, encouraging the employee to keep building on their skills and persistence, even if the immediate result isn't there yet.

Example of when results are more important: A seasoned salesperson, whose results have been declining recently. Despite being skilled, the employee has been coasting, relying on past success. As the leader, you focus on the result, showing the impact of declining numbers and reinforcing that the expected result needs to be met. Here, the conversation is about aligning effort to the performance standards that drive the business forward.

Keeping an eye on the balance between the factors can maintain motivation and fuel discretionary effort.

But to truly ignite motivation, it's essential to understand what drives each individual at a deeper level. This brings us to the *heart of motivation*—the distinction between intrinsic and extrinsic motivators. While motivation can boil down to finding meaning in the work, the source of that meaning can come from within or from external rewards.

THE HEART OF MOTIVATION

Human behavior is driven by two powerful forces: intrinsic and extrinsic motivation. Both are essential, but they affect behavior and performance in different ways. Knowing when and how to leverage each is key to driving lasting results. To truly ignite lasting motivation in others, it's important to understand how these forces work—and how they can either propel or hinder your leadership efforts.

Intrinsic motivators are internal factors that come from within an individual. They are the fuel that propels someone forward because they genuinely enjoy and receive satisfaction from the activity itself.

My husband loves gardening. In the spring and summer, he rushes home from work, changes his clothes, and starts work in the garden. He does it simply for pleasure—he prioritizes it (to my disdain, at times!) and has a lot of energy for it. In the winter, he plans all of his next year's gardening projects. There is no external factor that influences how he feels about gardening; it is a purely internal trigger.

Extrinsic motivation, on the other hand, comes from external factors. This is when we do something because of the reward we gain from it, such as recognition, awards, or money. For instance, when our friends compliment our garden during a backyard gathering, that's an extrinsic reward.

In the workplace, examples of external motivators include pay increases, bonuses, public recognition, and perks like free meals.

THE LIMITS OF MONETARY MOTIVATION

Maybe you remember a memorable scene from *Mad Men*, where Don Draper is talking to Peggy Olson. Peggy, frustrated by her lack of recognition, confronts Don about her contributions, and he responds bluntly, "That's what the money is for!"

There was a time when a paycheck alone was deemed a sufficient motivator. Believe it or not, from time to time I still hear, "They should be motivated by the paycheck," suggesting that financial compensation on its own should fuel drive and dedication. That landscape has evolved dramatically. The truth we've come to understand is that engagement transcends the transactional.

I want to double-click on why money has its limits because it always comes up when I teach this Function in my workshops. There is a prevalent belief that money serves as the ultimate motivator, but in reality, it's more complex. Yes, pay needs to be fair, based on the work that is done and market conditions. Period. If employees perceive that this is not so, the leader must clarify this misconception or the issue will impact engagement. As Daniel Pink says in his book *Drive*, "Take the issue of money off the table."[2]

Ensure that employees are paid enough so they are not distracted by financial concerns and can focus on the work itself and the internal motivators that drive deeper satisfaction and engagement. This doesn't imply that money is unimportant, but rather, beyond a certain point, additional financial incentives do not significantly enhance motivation and can sometimes even diminish it. I work with a lot of people who stay in jobs they don't really like; on teams, they don't click with or feel disconnected from the organization's mission simply because the pay is good. Every day they feel like they are climbing Everest, albeit wearing more expensive hiking boots. But it's still an effort.

Dependency on monetary rewards can become a relentless pursuit for more, often masking deeper and real desires for recognition, autonomy, and a sense of purpose. Ironically, when employees ask for higher pay, they might actually be seeking more intrinsic rewards, but through a more socially acceptable route. It's easier to ask for more money than to ask for recognition, or positive feedback, or greater responsibility.

---

2   Daniel H. Pink, *Drive: The Surprising Truth About What Motivates Us* (Riverhead Books, 2011), 33.

In addressing motivation, leaders must recognize the limitations of financial rewards as a long-term motivator. Instead, shift the focus toward balancing fair pay with a culture that values personal growth, meaningful work, and a sense of belonging. Create and cultivate a workplace where motivation is driven not by the desire for a bigger paycheck but by the rewarding nature of the work itself. This not only increases job satisfaction but also builds a team that is genuinely committed and engaged, willing to contribute their best to collective success.

The bottom line is people want work that feels meaningful and fulfilling. They want to grow, feel connected to a bigger purpose, and enjoy being part of a team. When these needs are met, employees don't just show up for the paycheck; they show up because they love what they do.

Here's the key: While extrinsic motivators are important, as we'll discuss, to ignite motivation leaders must tap into intrinsic motivators. They have many options for energizing internal drivers such as a sense of purpose, growth, and autonomy. And the best part? They don't require money to activate.

Intrinsic motivators have a lasting impact, yielding higher levels of job fulfillment, creativity, and engagement. When leaders focus on intrinsic motivators, they create a deeper connection to the work, resulting in motivation that endures and fuels sustained performance.

By contrast, extrinsic motivators have a shorter life cycle. They may energize in the moment, but as time passes, the motivation wanes. Consider a bonus. When we receive it, we feel great—like we're valued and appreciated. But once the money is spent, the boost it provides tends to dissipate, and day-to-day work might no longer feel as rewarding until the next bonus nears.

Extrinsic motivators have their place, without a doubt. Many of my clients offer free perks like weekly or monthly lunches to their employees. It is a way to bring people into the office, build relationships, and give employees opportunities to network and foster a sense of belonging. This is very important, but there is a risk. Over time, these perks become expected and lose their motivational power. For example, a pizza lunch on the last Friday of each month is a great way to bring the team together, but no one on the team says, "I'm going to work a little harder and give my discretionary effort because I'll get pizza at the end of the month."

Pizza lunches and similar rewards serve their purpose, but they can't be the sole strategy for team motivation. What if budget cuts occur and the pizza lunches go away? That's a huge demotivator. The sudden absence of a once-expected reward can have a negative impact.

I'm not suggesting you don't do pizza lunches or other extrinsic motivators, only that you change them from time to time so they don't become expected norms. Vary your benefits and give really good reasons as to the purpose they serve.

Combining intrinsic and extrinsic motivators can create a more enduring and impactful source of motivation. Employees feel personally invested in their work through intrinsic factors like growth and purpose, and receiving extrinsic rewards and recognition for their achievements reinforces their efforts. Let's look at how this can work in practice:

Intrinsic—Personal growth plans: Imagine an employee collaborating with their manager to create a personalized growth plan. This plan is aligned with the employee's career aspirations and personal interests, providing a sense of purpose and direction. It taps into intrinsic motivation by focusing on the employee's desire for self-improvement and mastery.

Extrinsic—Career advancement opportunities: To complement this, the manager also outlines clear paths for career advancement within the company, offering the potential for promotions or transitions to new roles with greater responsibility. This provides the extrinsic reward—concrete steps toward financial gain or higher status.

The intrinsic desire for growth is matched by external opportunities for recognition and advancement.

Or

Intrinsic—Autonomy in projects: An employee is given the autonomy to propose and lead a project related to an area they are passionate about. This gives them a sense of ownership and control over their work, nurturing their intrinsic need for autonomy and creativity.

Extrinsic—Public recognition and rewards: The employee's successful completion of the project is then recognized publicly during a company-wide meeting. Additionally, they are offered a tangible reward such as a performance bonus or extra vacation days.

The intrinsic motivation to innovate is reinforced by external recognition and a financial reward, showing that both their efforts and results matter.

When you have the opportunity to combine intrinsic and extrinsic motivators, seize it. Together, they can be a powerful tool for driving sustained performance and deeper engagement. That said, the focus should always lean toward intrinsic motivators. These are the heart of motivation—the real drivers of long-term engagement and performance.

UNCOVERING INTRINSIC MOTIVATORS

In this section, we will explore how to identify those deeper, intrinsic motivators that ignite lasting engagement. But first, let's go back to the first pillar of intentional leadership: self-awareness. Understanding what motivates you is important because we have a tendency to fish with strawberries—to impose our own motivators on others.

Here is an exercise that might shed light on your current motivation practices. Review the list of motivators below and check off the ones in the "Me" column that resonate with you at this moment in time. The trick is to keep it to a maximum of five. Yup, it's hard, but you need to be clear about what your true motivators are. Of course, we can be motivated by many more, but which ones are you less willing to negotiate over right now?

When you've completed the "Me" column, let's shift to situational awareness. Again, go through the same process for a direct report (DR#1), perhaps focusing on someone you think may need a motivation boost. What do you think is important to them? Select five. Repeat if you have more direct reports.

MOTIVATOR	ME	DR#1	DR#2	DR#3
Achievement				
Autonomy				
Boldness				
Challenge				
Change				
Competence				
Completion				
Creativity				
Curiosity				
Expertise				
Fun				
Growth				
High Standards				
Impact				
Learning				
Mastery				
Money				
Problem-Solving				
Progress				
Promotion				
Purpose				
Recognition				
Relationships				
Results				
Risk-taking				
Self-expression				
Stability				
Structure				
Support				

After completing this exercise, compare the motivators you've identified for yourself and your direct reports. Are there similarities? If so, are you fishing with strawberries? In other words, are you letting your motivators blind you to what actually motivates your team members?

If you identified motivators for your direct reports, but are not sure what to do with them, that's okay. Take time to think about how you can incorporate what they need with what they do.

For example, if one of the motivators you identified is achievement, reflect on whether the employee has ambitious, but attainable goals. Do you provide stretch assignments and acknowledge their accomplishments?

If self-expression is a motivator for one of your team members, consider if the individual has opportunities to share their ideas and opinions. Can you encourage them to contribute to brainstorming sessions or take ownership of projects where they can put their personal stamp on the work?

If you had a hard time figuring out what motivates your team members, don't worry; the next section will guide you through strategies to help you uncover those hidden motivators.

OBSERVE YOUR PEOPLE

There are three key areas where you, as a leader, can observe your employees, reflect on how they respond, and get insights about their intrinsic motivators:

1. **Energy levels:** Notice when you see an abundance of energy. What tasks and activities seem to energize them? Which ones drain them? For example, you notice that Aiysha lights up during brainstorming sessions and actively contributes

ideas. She seems energized and engaged when the team is working on creative problem-solving tasks. However, when it comes to routine administrative work, she often looks drained and less enthusiastic. This suggests that Aiysha is motivated by creative and dynamic work rather than repetitive tasks.

2. **Quality of work:** Observe when their work is of high quality and when it falls short. What conditions lead to these outcomes? For example, Bruce consistently delivers high-quality reports when he has clear deadlines and well-defined objectives. His attention to detail and thoroughness shine through when he knows exactly what is expected. However, when given open-ended tasks without clear guidelines, his work tends to be less polished, indicating that Bruce thrives in structured environments with clear expectations.

3. **Avoidance:** Identify what tasks or responsibilities your team members tend to avoid. People generally avoid or procrastinate on things they don't like doing. For example, you've noticed that Nia tends to procrastinate on tasks that involve complex data analysis, often pushing them to the last minute or finding reasons to delay. However, she eagerly volunteers for client-facing activities and excels in those roles. This avoidance behavior suggests that Nia may find data-heavy tasks unmotivating or intimidating, while she is more motivated by interactions and relationship building.

You've observed your team members at their highs and lows. Now what? It's always a good practice to validate your insights by getting curious and asking good questions during one-on-ones, or when coaching.

ASK PROBING QUESTIONS

You're in a one-on-one meeting with one of your team members, Kairin. She's been doing well, but you sense there's more potential that hasn't been tapped into yet. You start with the usual questions: "How's everything going?" "Anything you need help with?"

Kairin gives you polite, surface-level answers. But you know there's more beneath the surface—something that could ignite her motivation and take her performance to the next level. The challenge is figuring out what that is.

That's the true art of asking thought-provoking open-ended questions. Your goal is to dig deeper, to uncover what truly drives your team members—beyond the obvious answers.

Instead of asking, "What motivates you?"—which can often lead to generic or rehearsed responses—try asking questions that invite reflection and storytelling. Here are some examples, along with insights into what the answers can tell you:

- *"What was the best part of last week? Why?"* This question encourages your team member to think about a recent positive experience and articulate what made it meaningful. In Kairin's case, you might discover that she felt energized after collaborating on a project, which could point to a motivator like teamwork or creative problem-solving.
- *"What did you learn?"* This question is a subtle way of asking what excites them intellectually. If Kairin lights up talking about a new skill or piece of knowledge she gained, it might suggest that she's motivated by learning and growth.
- *"What task or part of last week was the most draining? Why?"* Understanding what drains your team members is just as important as knowing what energizes them. If Kairin shares

that she felt overwhelmed by repetitive tasks, this could indicate a need for variety or more challenging work.

- *"What are you most proud of?"* This question helps you understand what Kairin values in her work. If she's proud of a detailed report she created, she might be motivated by precision and excellence.
- *"When did you have an abundance of energy?"* This question zeroes in on what tasks or situations naturally energize her. If Kairin says she felt most energized during a brainstorming session, that suggests that she thrives in creative environments.
- *"What have you done recently that made you the most frustrated?"* Frustration can be a window into unmet needs or misaligned tasks. If Kairin mentions a lack of clear direction, that might mean she's motivated by structure and clarity.
- *"What were some speed bumps that got in your way?"* This helps identify obstacles that hinder motivation. If Kairin mentions issues with team communication, that could highlight a need for better collaboration or support.

The idea is that you keep probing to uncover how people feel about the work they do—good and bad. By asking these types of questions, you're not simply gathering information; you're opening a dialogue that helps your team members reflect on what truly drives them. The key is to keep the conversation flowing, gently nudging for more specific answers and showing genuine curiosity. Sometimes the most revealing answers come from the most unexpected question.

Note that our motivators can change over time, or we might prioritize some over others in different phases of our lives, so it's important to regularly engage in this process of observing, reflecting, and questioning.

PERSONALITY TRAITS AND INTRINSIC MOTIVATORS

Remember our four team members with different styles from the previous chapter? Using the DiSC framework gives you a window into what might motivate your direct reports intrinsically. Each DiSC style—Dominance (D), Influence (i), Steadiness (S), and Conscientiousness (C)—carries unique preferences, fears, and motivators. By aligning tasks and roles with these intrinsic motivators, you can significantly enhance engagement and satisfaction. You can also avoid fishing with strawberries and instead offer the right bait for each employee's unique motivators.

Let's start with the D style. That would be me. D style individuals want results fast, are direct, and are task-focused.

Intrinsic motivators: Challenges, autonomy, and quick results. Those with a D style are motivated by tasks that allow them to see immediate outcomes. They thrive on overcoming obstacles and enjoy autonomy in how they achieve their goals.

Examples: Assign them to lead high-stakes projects with critical deadlines. Encourage them to set ambitious goals for themselves and the team. Provide opportunities for independent work where they can exercise control over the outcome.

Your i style employees want results in a different, unique way and are people-focused.

Intrinsic motivators: Social recognition, collaboration, and influence. Individuals with an i style are energized by interacting with others and being in the spotlight. They seek environments where they can express their ideas freely and influence decisions.

Examples: Involve them in brainstorming sessions for new initiatives. Assign roles that enhance their visibility within the organization, such as leading presentations or representing the team in cross-functional meetings.

S style individuals, often described as team players, are people-focused.

Intrinsic motivators: Harmony, stability, and cooperation. S style employees find motivation in consistent environments where teamwork and support are emphasized. They appreciate recognition for their loyalty and dedication.

Examples: Engage them in roles that require steady effort and collaboration, such as maintaining client relationships or managing long-term projects. Recognize their contributions to team cohesion and provide a stable work environment that minimizes sudden changes.

C style people tend to be analytical, detail-oriented, and task-focused.

Intrinsic motivators: Accuracy, knowledge, and independence. C styles are driven by opportunities to use their expertise to solve complex problems. They value precision and are motivated by roles that allow them to apply their analytical skills.

Examples: Assign them to tasks that require detailed analysis and strategic planning, such as data analysis or process optimization projects. Encourage their pursuit of professional development to deepen their expertise.

Using personality assessments to uncover motivators can spark a great conversation, build awareness for both the leader and the follower, and forge a stronger bond. And make sure to share your own results. Vulnerability fosters trust and encourages a more open, authentic exchange.

One word of caution: personality assessments are not intended to pigeonhole people; they are tools to help us understand ourselves and others. They are simply tools, and there is more to us than our styles.

IGNITE MOTIVATION SUMMARY

This chapter explores the essential connection between motivation and engagement, highlighting how a leader's role is to ignite motivation rather than simply "give" it. By understanding the balance between intrinsic and extrinsic motivators, leaders can create an environment where employees are inspired to give their discretionary effort, achieve goals, and find their true potential. As Zig Zigler's quote reminds us, motivation is not a one-time effort—it requires regular attention and renewal.

Why Ignite Motivation

Here are the top three reasons to focus on igniting motivation in your people:

- **Boosts engagement and discretionary effort:** Motivated employees are more engaged and willing to put in extra effort, which directly impacts productivity and team performance.
- **Fosters long-term fulfillment:** Intrinsic motivation leads to deeper job satisfaction, creativity, and a greater sense of purpose, making employees more committed to their roles.

- **Improves organizational outcomes:** Motivation is the fuel for engagement, which is the driving force behind innovation, retention, and organizational success.

When to Ignite Motivation

It's important to ignite motivation at all times, but especially:

- When morale is low, and employees seem disengaged or passive
- When tasks are not completed to the expected standard or on time
- When team members are procrastinating or showing signs of burnout

How to Ignite Motivation

Here are some of the most effective tactics for igniting motivation:

- **Observe and ask:** Get to know your people and what motivates them.
- **Avoid assumptions:** Don't project your own motivators. Remember strawberries!
- **Focus on intrinsic:** Learn what is important on the inside.
- **Balance with extrinsic:** Complement intrinsic with extrinsic for sustainability.
- **Customize the approach:** Tailor motivation strategies to individual team members' DiSC profiles or other personality assessments.
- **Recognize effort and result:** Ensure that both effort and results are acknowledged, understanding that the balance between the two can drive or diminish motivation.

YOUR CHALLENGE

After digesting this chapter, your assignment is to become an observer for a week. Note instances where the team members show high engagement and energy, as well as moments where they seem drained or less motivated.

In addition, learn two key intrinsic motivators for each member of your team. You can do this during your one-on-ones, through informal conversations, or by observation. Make sure you are not making any assumptions and fishing with strawberries without realizing it.

Finally, choose one team member you believe could benefit from a motivation boost. Engage in a one-on-one conversation with them, aiming to discover (not assume) their unique motivators. Use open-ended questions that go beyond the surface, such as "What aspect of your work do you find most fulfilling?" or "Can you tell me about a time when you felt highly motivated at work? What sparked it?" Find opportunities to align the work of the team member with what motivates them. Let's say one of their motivators is social connection. Assign them tasks that allow them to be collaborative and lean on others. Or if you discover that a motivator is creativity, allow them to tackle a problem plaguing the team that calls for a creative solution.

Two of the greatest motivators for employees in the modern workplace are growth and development. That's great news for any leader reading this book because the next function is all about—you guessed it—talent development.

Chapter Six

DEVELOP TALENT

"The growth and development of people is the highest calling of leadership."

—HARVEY S. FIRESTONE

Seriously, can we hit pause for a second? I admit that I geek out over leadership stuff, but this quote? Shivers! And Harvey Firestone, the founder of Firestone Tire and Rubber Company, said that a century ago!

The work you do as a leader isn't just about the bottom line or hitting quarterly targets; it's about investing in people, recognizing their potential, and guiding them toward success. Leadership, in its purest form, is about fostering growth and enabling individuals to meet and exceed their own expectations. It's about creating an environment where talent can flourish, challenges become opportunities for development, and the journey of growth is a shared one. The legacy of a leader is often seen in the success and advancement of their team members long after projects are completed or goals are achieved.

The beauty of development is its simplicity and accessibility.

It doesn't require grand gestures or elaborate plans. It only needs attentiveness, genuine interest in a person, and a commitment to nurturing talents. By weaving development into daily work life, you transform it from a formal, annual event into a natural, continuous journey of growth. The essence of development lies in the everyday interactions, feedback sessions, one-on-one meetings, and even casual conversations that occur organically. The goal is to reach a place where coaching, mentoring, and creating learning and development opportunities are so natural and common that they're part of your leadership DNA.

In this chapter, we'll explore how you can build the competencies your team members need to meet current demands while also preparing them for future challenges. By focusing on continuous growth and skill development, you're optimizing productivity today and laying the groundwork for sustained performance and innovation tomorrow.

THE CASE FOR TALENT DEVELOPMENT

Since the pandemic, I have received a surge of requests from clients for career coaching. I think this trend reflects individuals' heightened need to find greater fulfillment, purpose, and meaning in the work they do. Which I totally love! It is so encouraging that people are not willing to simply go through the motions of life. That they desire to take control where they can and actively work toward a better outcome for themselves. Life is too short!

The global pandemic has acted as a catalyst for introspection for many, prompting questions about life, career satisfaction, purpose, and what truly matters. This has driven individuals to seek out career coaching as a tool for creating paths that align more closely with their values and aspirations.

Other factors contribute to this trend as well. Firstly, the digital revolution and automation have rapidly changed the nature of many jobs, requiring new skills and competencies. Employees find themselves at a crossroads, eager to adapt but unsure of the direction to take. Secondly, the generational shift in the workforce, with millennials and Gen Z now forming a significant percentage, introduces new values into the professional sphere. These younger employees prioritize meaningful work, personal growth, and work-life balance more than previous generations, driving them to careers that align with their broader life goals.

In this context, the role of leaders in developing talent has never been more critical. The demand for career coaching demonstrates the need for leaders to become facilitators of growth, helping their team members navigate their careers with intention and insight. It's more than managing; it's mentoring, guiding, and empowering employees to unlock their full potential.

Many leaders hold a narrow perspective of the true value of talent development. It is too often directly linked with career advancement, when there actually are many other reasons to develop people: to increase engagement, improve agility, and more. Hanging onto this one-dimensional view prevents leaders and organizations from utilizing the full potential of this Function.

Let's broaden our perspective. There are four critical reasons why organizations need to grow and develop their people:

1. To promote engagement and retention
2. As a means of fostering agility and change
3. To prompt or spur innovation and creativity
4. For future leader development

Let's briefly discuss each.

ENGAGEMENT AND RETENTION

As we explored in the last chapter, "engagement" is not simply a buzzword. It is the heartbeat of organizational health and success. When employees are engaged, they tend to stick around. How do we know talent development is an engagement driver? Well, because employees ask for it. Here are some stats from Gallup:[3]

- Fifty-seven percent of employees want to update their skills.
- Forty-eight percent of employees would consider switching their jobs in order to upskill.
- Employees between the ages of eighteen and twenty-four consider upskilling their job's most important benefit.
- Fifty-three percent of workers aged fifty-five and older say upskilling is "very" or "extremely" important.

More than half of the employees surveyed said they want to update their skills, and almost half of them said they would leave their jobs to do it. Not to be dramatic, but imagine half of your team leaving because they had better opportunities to grow in other places.

But what if you spend the time and money to grow your people, and they leave your team? Consider the alternative: What if you don't develop them and they stay? The real risk is ending up with team members who don't have the skills to fully contribute to the success of the organization. Richard Branson captured the essence of this dilemma: "Train people well enough so they can leave, treat them well enough so they don't want to."[4]

---

3   Scott Miller, "How to Win the 'Great Resignation,'" Gallup, November 1, 2021, https://www.gallup.com/workplace/356729/win-great-resignation.aspx#.

4   Richard Branson (@richardbranson), "Train people well enough so they can leave, treat them well enough so they don't want to http://virg.in/lys," Twitter (now X), March 27, 2014, https://x.com/richardbranson/status/449220072176107520?lang=en.

AGILITY AND CHANGE

Remember Kodak? If you don't, that's kind of the point. If you do, you know that the company delayed in adapting to digital photography, which allowed competitors to enter and dominate the market, leaving Kodak in the dust. Agility and nimbleness are the key drivers of competitive advantage.

What is the key to organizational agility? A diverse skill inventory. The broader the collection of skills, the easier it is for a team to adjust, shift, and leverage opportunities that meet market demands and make companies more agile.

Recall Rose, from earlier chapters, the television executive brought in to transform the network's digital broadcasting. One of the reasons the transition was slow, long, and painful was because her organization didn't have the necessary skills to efficiently navigate the change. Employees had to be trained and new talent hired, impacting the speed to execution.

INNOVATION AND CREATIVITY

How does talent development impact innovation and creativity? It's simple: development breaks down the walls of routine thinking, pushing teams beyond the "this is how we've always done it" mindset to explore new territories.

When people are exposed to new experiences and learn new methods or technologies, they start seeing problems through a new lens, sparking creative solutions—an idea so well captured in Oliver Wendell Holmes Sr.'s quote: "Every now and then a man's mind is stretched by a new idea or sensation, and never shrinks back to its former dimensions."[5]

---

5   Oliver Wendell Holmes, "The Autocrat of the Breakfast-Table: Every Man His Own Boswell," *The Atlantic*, September 1858, 502.

Pixar Animation Studios, renowned for its innovative storytelling and pioneering technology in animation, is strongly committed to talent development through its Pixar University, a professional development program that offers courses ranging from drawing and painting to storytelling and cinematography. This investment in continuous learning encourages employees to think creatively and collaborate across disciplines, leading to groundbreaking films that push the boundaries of what is possible in animation. Each new skill acquired by its team contributes to a rich, creative environment where original ideas flourish, showcasing how nurturing talent directly enhances innovation and creativity.

FUTURE LEADER DEVELOPMENT

The leaders of tomorrow are developed today. Talent development builds a pipeline of capable people ready to lead teams, make strategic decisions, and drive the company's success. One of my clients, a four-hundred person tech company, has a policy that no one can get promoted to a leadership role at any level unless they have a successor. That's a bold policy! And I love it. It forces leaders to prioritize development because it impacts their own progress.

Why is future leader development important? For one, it safeguards organizational knowledge. As experienced leaders move on, their accumulated knowledge and insights can be lost if there isn't a new generation ready to step in and carry the torch. By focusing on talent development, you're not just preparing someone to fill a position—you're preserving the wisdom, culture, and strategic insight that make your organization unique.

Furthermore, when employees see internal promotions, they

realize there is a clear path for growth and development within the company, and they are more likely to be engaged and committed to their work. This, in turn, reduces turnover and builds a strong, cohesive team that is ready to tackle future challenges.

DEVELOPMENT ROLES AND RESPONSIBILITIES

I am about to blow your mind! Here goes: growing and developing your team members is not your responsibility.

While you, as a leader, play a crucial role in your team's growth, you are part of a broader ecosystem involving the organization and employees themselves. If you feel the heaviness of development on your shoulders, you can shed some of the weight now.

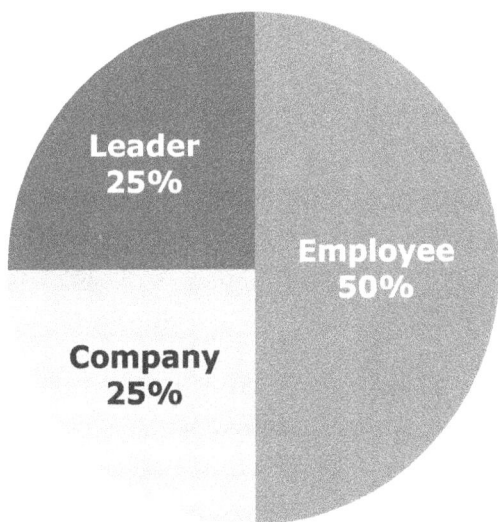

As this graphic shows, employees are responsible for 50 percent of their development, the organization 25 percent, and you, the leader, the other 25 percent.

If companies want to drive engagement and leverage the benefits of talent development, they need to empower employees to manage their own development, to own it so they can be accountable for it. The days of leaders deciding behind closed doors where people move and what is the best for them are over.

I deliver a lot of "Design Your Career" workshops to teach and empower employees to take charge of their careers. And I constantly hear from participants that either the manager or the organization will decide where they will go next.

What? That's ridiculous.

Of course we need to stretch our people and give them opportunities to explore and learn, but this needs to be in collaboration and aligned with the employee's desired development. After all, it is their life.

During PDP (personal development plan) time, it's common for leaders to fill out the required forms on behalf of their employees. Don't do that! It may be faster to fill out the PDP and send it to HR, but is that an example of your highest calling? Anyway, enough preaching, you get it.

Dividing the responsibilities of development between the employee, the organization, and the leader empowers employees to take ownership of their growth, gives leaders structure for how to support their team members effectively, and ensures that the organization creates the right environment for learning and development to thrive.

Let's explore the roles and responsibilities.

EMPLOYEE RESPONSIBILITIES

While leaders play a crucial role in guiding and supporting development, the real progress comes when employees take ownership of their growth. Ownership comes from involvement.

We can't expect to fully commit to something if we haven't been part of shaping it from the beginning. The same is true for growth and development—employees must take the lead in their career paths, with the support of their leaders and the organization.

Here are the key responsibilities employees need to own in their development:

- **Gain self-awareness:** Regularly evaluate strengths, weaknesses, and areas for improvement. Understand growth areas.
- **Seek feedback:** Proactively ask for positive and constructive feedback from their manager, peers, and greater network.
- **Research development opportunities:** Continuously explore potential career paths. Research, ask questions, and seek out information on various ways to develop.
- **Set goals:** Clearly define specific, achievable career goals.
- **Communication aspirations:** Share career aspirations and development plans with their manager. Ask for support.
- **Track progress:** Ensure plans are executed and revised if required. Communicate progress with their manager.
- **Build a network:** Connect with peers, mentors, and leaders across different departments to build a web of interdependence that opens doors to new ideas, a pool of skills, and expertise.
- **Make decisions:** Ultimately, make career decisions with guidance and support from their leader.
- **Engage in learning:** Actively seek and participate in opportunities for learning—whether it's formal training, workshops, or on-the-job experiences.

While the idea of employees taking ownership of their career development might seem intuitive, the reality is that workplaces haven't traditionally operated with the employee in the driver's seat and the leader as the GPS, guiding the way. Making this happen requires a mindset shift for both leaders and employees. Leaders need to start by setting clear expectations.

Here's an example of a conversation to ensure the employee understands their role and responsibilities and is ready to take the lead in their development.

> **Leader:** "I'd like to discuss your development and how we can work together on it. While I'm here to support and guide you, I want you to own at least fifty percent of the journey. The organization and I each have a part to play, but you ultimately drive your growth. How do you feel about that?"

> **Employee:** "Sounds good. Where do I start?"

> **Leader:** "Great! The first step is to think about where you see your career going. Have you considered what areas you want to develop or where you'd like to be in the next couple of years?"

> **Employee:** "I've been thinking a lot about where I want to go. I'm interested in project management, but I'm not sure how to get there."

> **Leader:** "That's interesting. Why project management? What about it appeals to you?"

> **Employee:** "I really enjoy working on projects, coordinating tasks, and making sure everything comes together on time. I like keeping track of progress and helping others on the team stay organized. Plus, I've seen how effective project managers make a big difference in how work gets done."

Leader: "It sounds like you have a natural interest in bringing structure and organization to projects. It's great that you are thinking in that direction. Project management skills could certainly help you build on those strengths and make a big impact on the team."

Employee: "Yeah, that's what I'm hoping for."

Leader: "So where do you think you can start?"

Employee: "I can explore specific skills and experiences I'll need to develop in that area. I can research training programs and connect with our PMO to get more insights. Perhaps I can find a mentor or job-shadow a project manager."

Leader: "Solid ideas. Why don't you do the research and let's plan together for how you can develop this skill. Part of your responsibility is seeking out these learning opportunities and feedback. I'll support you by providing resources and facilitating connections within the organization."

Employee: "That sounds great. I will draft a plan for us to review."

Leader: "We'll review it together in our next one-on-one meeting. And this is an ongoing conversation. We'll regularly check in on your progress and adjust the plan as needed."

Even though the employee takes the lead in driving their development, the organization provides the structure and support needed to shape that journey. Let's explore how great organizations offer guidance to help their people grow.

ORGANIZATION RESPONSIBILITIES

The organization as a whole is tasked with supporting an employee's development. What follows are some of the ways great companies support their people and give them what they need to grow. If your organization isn't offering these, consider how you, as a leader, can advocate for these resources or take initiative to fill the gaps.

Clear vision, direction, strategy, and business plans for the future: When there is clarity and transparency, employees can align their aspirations and create more meaningful career paths for themselves. For example, in a company where the vision is to become a leader in sustainable packaging, employees can tailor their development to align with this direction. A marketing employee might focus on gaining expertise in eco-friendly branding, while a product designer might seek training in sustainable materials. By knowing the company's long-term goals, employees can make informed decisions about their own growth and how they contribute to the bigger picture.

Tools and resources to support development: Employees are sometimes expected to meet new challenges or goals, without the proper tools. For example, an organization may emphasize the importance of working collaboratively, but if employees aren't given access to the right collaboration software, like Slack or Miro, they'll struggle to communicate effectively and manage tasks across remote and in-office teams. Without these tools, the organization's expectations around collaboration can become frustrating or unachievable, limiting both individual and team performance.

Facilitation of learning and development opportunities for employees: Organizations should offer training courses, personal development budgets, mentorship programs, and job-shadowing initiatives, for example. And when employees are learning, they should be given the time to fully participate in these initiatives. You'd be surprised how often managers pull their people from training because something urgent comes up, sending the message that learning is not a priority.

As a leader, it's important to first look at what the organization offers to support your employees' development and use those resources to their full potential. But don't be discouraged if the company doesn't provide everything you need—there's still a lot within your power that you can leverage to help your people grow. Let's explore the key responsibilities you hold as a leader in guiding development.

LEADER RESPONSIBILITIES

Your role is to guide the way, being there for the employee as they take charge and direct the process and also pointing them toward the resources and opportunities the company offers. Guidance means several different things in this case, and each of these is broken out below.

Define direction: Regularly share insights about organizational strategies, ensuring employees understand how their roles connect with the company's direction. Translate the vision into reality. You are higher up and most likely have a different vantage point. Share what you can when you can.

A client in her twenties told me that two years into her career, she decided to plan her next steps. She met her HR business partner and signed up for the company mentorship program. Excited, she shared her goal and action plan with her leader and was met with, "Haven't you heard we're restructuring the business? We'll need to get back to you on potential opportunities."

That feeling of motivation and empowerment evaporated in

an instant. The moral is that, whenever possible, communicate with your team what's happening in the organization—on other teams, and, of course, your team. Make this a regular practice. Create a section in your monthly team meeting to share information that your team doesn't have access to.

Align objectives: Work to align employees' aspirations and capabilities with the organization's goals by identifying and nurturing development paths that benefit both the individual and the team. This means finding ways to connect what your employees want to achieve with how their growth can add value to the team and the company.

Build self-awareness: Help your employees understand their strengths and areas for growth by encouraging reflection and offering tools like personality assessments (DiSC, MBTI, etc.).

Provide feedback: Regularly offer positive and constructive feedback to facilitate employee self-awareness and drive their development. Consistent feedback is vital for career growth. We'll explore feedback in greater detail in Chapter Eight.

Create space: Dedicate time during one-on-ones for meaningful development conversations, creating a platform for open dialogue and planning. Be careful not to make assumptions about what your employees want. Get to know your people and give them the space to process what they know, where they want to go, and how to get there. Be curious and open. Ask questions. You have to know your people's aspirations and capabilities and align them with the company's direction.

Coach and mentor employees: Build business acumen, skills, and self-awareness, and identify learning and development opportunities that cater to individual growth needs and aspirations. As we will discuss in Chapter Eight, my simplified version of coaching and mentoring is to take someone from point A to point B in comfort.

Provide tools: Ensure employees have access to necessary resources, tools (such as those included in the "Employee Responsibilities" section), and opportunities for development, including training programs, mentorship, and project assignments. Build bridges by facilitating introductions and sharing existing corporate programs like training, mentorship, or special projects.

As a leader, your role in employee development is a critical one. While the employee owns 50 percent of their development and the organization 25 percent, the remaining 25 percent belongs to you and unlocks the door to meaningful growth.

Let's explore how you can make this process less arduous and more natural by examining strategies and specific skills that will help you support your team members' development with greater ease and confidence.

THE POWER OF ORGANIC CONVERSATIONS

Development isn't an event. It doesn't only happen during formal reviews or planned meetings. Rather, development opportunities can pop up in the most unexpected moments.

I witnessed the following conversation one Monday morning at a client's office while waiting for my turn to push the latte button.

Leader: "Hey, how was your weekend?"

Employee: "It was awesome."

Leader: "What did you do?"

Employee: "I coach in a children's hockey league, and my team played in the championship tournament."

Leader: "How did they do?"

Employee: "We came in second, which was a big surprise. The team came a long way."

Leader: "How did you get into coaching?"

Employee: "My son plays hockey, and I thought I'd get involved. Now, I love it! Coaching is a happy place in my life."

Leader: "What do you like about it?"

Employee: "Hmm, good question. I've never really thought about it. I guess I like taking each player and really understanding what connects them to hockey and the position they play. I work with that to teach them skills and give them opportunities to practice in a way that offers challenges and builds their abilities."

Leader: "That's very special. Do you have opportunities to do that here, at work?"

Employee: "Hmm, not really. I don't see how I can step into that here."

Leader: "How about we put that on our next one-on-one agenda to explore and see if there are opportunities for you to use this valuable gift."

Impromptu discussions like this, often driven by genuine curiosity and connection, help uncover the unique talents and aspirations of team members.

Don't be afraid if they seem peripheral to the primary task

at hand. Personal conversations are far from a waste of time and often yield profound insights and create stronger bonds. While there is a strong temptation to prioritize direct, task-focused communication, it's worth considering how a simple question like, "Where do you see yourself in five years?" pales in comparison to the organic, heartfelt conversations that uncover an employee's true drivers/skills/interests.

In our hybrid world, you need to be more intentional about fostering these types of organic dialogues. The goal is to reach a place where coaching, mentoring, and creating growth are natural and common. To support this, I've designed a framework that offers a clear, step-by-step career development path that gives employees a focused approach to their development and provides leaders a road map on how and what support to provide.

CAREER DEVELOPMENT IN ACTION

We've already covered the role of the employee in their development and the responsibilities that it entails. Now, let's look at how those responsibilities align with the five key steps of career development: self-awareness, growth opportunities, goal setting, planning, and tapping into dependencies.

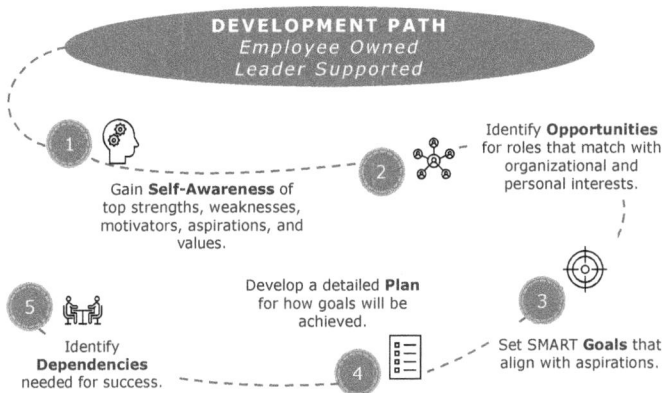

DEVELOPMENT PATH
Employee Owned
Leader Supported

1 — Gain **Self-Awareness** of top strengths, weaknesses, motivators, aspirations, and values.

2 — Identify **Opportunities** for roles that match with organizational and personal interests.

3 — Set SMART **Goals** that align with aspirations.

4 — Develop a detailed **Plan** for how goals will be achieved.

5 — Identify **Dependencies** needed for success.

In the following sections, I address each of these steps from the place where you stand as a leader. In other words, I'll suggest actions for you to take to guide your employees as they navigate their own career development.

STEP ONE: SELF-AWARENESS

The career development plan starts with self-awareness. As Socrates wisely said, "To know thyself is the beginning of wisdom." To create a path that leads to fulfilling and successful careers, employees must understand their strengths, weaknesses, demotivators, values, interests, and aspirations.

So what do you do? Create an environment where reflection, inquiry, and self-knowledge flourish. Guide them in the process of self-evaluation and equip them with tools to assess their own growth and chart their path forward.

To truly enable your team members to gain self-awareness, prioritize asking more and telling less. Thoughtful, open-ended questions encourage reflection and self-discovery, shifting the responsibility of growth to them and fostering greater self-reliance. It's not about providing all the answers—it's about guiding them to find those answers for themselves.

Again, I encourage leaders to have a portfolio of go-to questions. Not to go down the list, but as brainfood to prepare for and navigate conversations. Here are some of mine:

My favorite questions to explore strengths:

- Where and when do you consistently receive positive feedback?
- Can you describe a project or task where you felt highly effective?

- What skills do you think your colleagues would say you excel in?

For probing into weaknesses:

- In what areas do you feel you could use more training or education?
- Is there a task that you find more challenging than others? Why?
- What constructive feedback have you been given?

To uncover motivators:

- If you could do anything nonstop, what would it be?
- When you feel at your best, what are you doing?
- What kind of projects energize you and make you lose track of time?

To understand demotivators:

- What drains your energy?
- What do you procrastinate on?
- What would you stop doing if you could?

To dive into interests:

- If you had all the time in the world, what would you do? Why?
- What has recently piqued your curiosity? Why?
- What do you miss about your previous job?

To uncover values:

- Who do you admire? Why?
- What are your top three personal values? (Most people don't know their top values off the top of their head. If your employee does, validate that they're not just telling you what you want to hear.)
- What are you most proud of?

To crystallize aspirations:

- If you had more time, what would you want to learn?
- What impact do you want to have on this team, our organization, or the industry as a whole?
- Can you think of a person whose career trajectory you'd like to emulate?

I know I don't need to say this, but just in case: these are not meant to be asked all in one sitting. Having a good portfolio of open-ended go-to questions lets you stay in the flow of the discussion, just like in the chat about coaching hockey. Focus and stay in the moment, and ask follow-up questions—"why" and "tell-me-more" types of questions.

What your team member says is less important than giving them the space to think through the questions. One of the greatest gifts you can give your employees is the time to explore and articulate their insights, ideas, and desires. Often I hear from clients I coach how much they appreciate the insights I give them. This always makes me laugh because it seems the less I say and the more I ask questions, the more grateful they are!

Of course, leaders need to be open to change; what may be an aspiration today may not be tomorrow. I recently coached someone who wanted to move into a management role, and after leading a project for the team, decided to focus on developing Scrum Master skills instead. As people grow, their goals will evolve, and it's important to support them where they are.

Match Aspirations with Development Path

As you create space for your employees to crystallize their aspirations grounded in the reality of strengths, weaknesses, and opportunities, you help identify and support the right development path for each individual.

Remember fishing with strawberries? Just as we don't want to superimpose our motivators on our direct reports, the same goes for development. People view development in different ways depending on their needs and goals. Managers tell me that they can't develop their people because their organizations are flat, and they have no place to promote them. When I ask if the person wants to be promoted, the answer almost always is "Yes, of course, doesn't everyone!"

Well, no. Look, people want to move up in organizations, but that doesn't always take the form of a straight ascent. Sometimes, to get to the desired position, an individual might move sideways or even down to gain the experience they need so they can propel toward what they want. From my coaching sessions, I see that over 50 percent of people are not looking for the next rung on the ladder.

Michael Driver, PhD, a professor of organizational behavior at the University of Southern California, created a four-part framework for how people view development. Each of the four types—linear, expert, spiral, and transitory—is unique, and no single path is right for everyone. Understanding each allows you to tailor your approach and support your employee's aspirations.

As I walk through these, think about your direct reports and the paths they lean toward.

Linear Development

Often described as climbing the ladder, the Linear path is typically a sequential advancement through positions, increasing responsibility and complexity within the same field. Individuals on this development track aim to move vertically from entry-level roles to more senior positions, potentially culminating in leadership or executive roles.

In this model success is often measured by promotions, title changes, and the acquisition of broader managerial responsibilities. It emphasizes depth of expertise in a specific domain, leadership skills, and an increasing scope of influence within the organization.

How do you know if a team member is motivated by linear development? Look for a clear desire for promotions, taking initiative in roles that align with a hierarchical climb, and seeking opportunities to lead others.

For example, I worked with a leader, Shiv, who had a team member, Genevieve, who was eager to move up in the company. Genevieve constantly sought out leadership opportunities, volunteered to lead projects, and expressed interest in eventually taking on a management role.

Recognizing Genevieve's motivation for linear development, Shiv assigned her the responsibility of leading a high-visibility project. This gave Genevieve the chance to hone her leadership skills—such as influencing and motivating others—while helping her gain the reputation needed for her next promotion. By involving Genevieve in decision-making and connecting her with senior leaders across departments, Shiv provided experiences and mentorship that prepared her, in part, for the next level in her career.

To support team members like Genevieve on a Linear development path, you can use specific actions that cater directly to their desire for upward mobility and leadership experience. Here are a few tailored strategies:

1. **Assign leadership responsibilities:** Offer opportunities for the employee to lead projects or initiatives, providing them with informal leadership experiences. For instance, put them in charge when you are away or allow them to manage a small team on a project.
2. **Delegate decision-making authority:** Give them chances to make decisions that have an impact on the team or department, helping them build confidence and competence in leadership roles.
3. **Create stretch assignments:** Challenge them with assignments that require them to step outside their current comfort zone or level of responsibility, fostering growth in skills that will be crucial for their next role.
4. **Facilitate networking opportunities:** Encourage them to build relationships with senior leaders or other departments, which can expose them to new perspectives and help them prepare for future roles.
5. **Connect with a mentor:** Pair them with a mentor who has successfully navigated a linear career path. This mentor can provide guidance, share experiences, and help them strategize for the next steps in their career.

By incorporating these strategies, leaders can provide meaningful support for employees on a Linear development path, helping them build the skills and experiences necessary to move up within the organization.

Linear development can be challenging when there are limited opportunities for advancement. As a leader, it's important to develop your team members with the intent of movement, even when a promotion isn't immediately available. By growing their leadership skills and broadening their experiences, you prepare them for the next opportunity when it arises, even if it's outside of your area or organization.

Expert Development

This path is about becoming a subject matter expert or a specialist in a certain area, which could range from technical skills—like software development or engineering—to functional expertise in fields like marketing or finance.

Individuals pursuing this type of development are primarily motivated by mastery of their craft. They seek to continuously expand their knowledge, stay abreast of the latest developments in their field, and contribute significantly to their area of specialization. Success on this path is measured by their depth of expertise, recognition as an authority in their field, and their work's impact on their organization.

Tariq, a team leader at a tech company, had a team member, Leila, known for her strong command of cybersecurity. Leila expressed interest in continuing to learn and build her skills, and always stayed on top of the latest developments in the field. Recognizing Leila's drive for expert development, Tariq took several steps to support her growth.

First, he encouraged Leila to carve out dedicated time

during her week for research and self-study. Tariq understood that staying ahead in a rapidly evolving field like cybersecurity required consistent learning, and he made sure that Leila had the flexibility to focus on strengthening her skills. To build on this, he provided Leila with a personal development budget, which she could use to acquire specialized training. After all, she was in the best position to know what she needed. Recognizing Leila's ambition, Tariq worked with her to set stretch goals and challenged her to think critically about not just her own growth but also the team's.

Just like Tariq did with Leila, you can incorporate several strategies into the Expert development path:

1. **Allow dedicated learning time:** Allocate specific time during work hours for employees to focus on learning and deepening their expertise, whether through research, self-study, or online courses.

2. **Challenge them to innovate:** Encourage critical thinking by posing questions like, "What would take this to the next level?" or "How can we push the boundaries of what's been done before?" This prompts them to seek innovative solutions in their area of expertise.

3. **Provide a learning budget:** Offer a personal development budget for employees to select their own learning opportunities, such as attending industry conferences, subscribing to professional journals, or taking specialized courses.

4. **Encourage expertise sharing:** Create opportunities for them to share their expertise with the team through internal workshops, presentations, or mentoring. This reinforces their knowledge and fosters a culture of continuous learning.

5. **Promote independent projects:** Encourage employees to propose and lead independent projects that allow them to

experiment and apply new knowledge or techniques, fostering creativity and deep learning.

6. **Set stretch goals:** Collaborate with them to set ambitious yet achievable goals that push their expertise to the next level, ensuring continuous growth.

By incorporating these strategies, you help create an environment where mastery is valued and continuous learning becomes the norm. Nurture their passion for their craft, and you'll unlock their potential to make a lasting impact.

Spiral Development

Okay, I don't love that name. "Spiral development" sounds like something that goes round and round without getting anywhere, right? But this path represents the dynamic process of learning different functions within one area of the business, which is actually quite exciting. Think of it as career exploration with a purpose—where every rotation gives the employee a new perspective and a deeper understanding of how everything fits together.

Spiral development is ideal for those who aren't quite ready to commit to a specific leadership path or area of expertise. Instead, these individuals are eager to explore a range of roles to discover where their strengths and passions truly lie.

After graduating from university, my son Tom started his career in marketing. Like many recent graduates, he wasn't entirely sure which specific area of marketing he wanted to specialize in. His first few years were all about exploration and gaining exposure to different facets of the marketing world. Rather than diving deep into one niche, Tom was eager to get a taste of everything—from content marketing and social media strategy to digital advertising and market research.

What Tom needed was exposure to various roles and responsibilities across different teams. This wasn't about jumping into leadership just yet—it was about broadening his horizons. He worked with the content marketing team for a few months, helping them develop campaign strategies. Then, he rotated to digital marketing, where he collaborated on paid advertising initiatives and learned how to optimize campaigns for performance. After that, he spent time with the market research team, analyzing consumer data and drawing insights that could guide the overall marketing strategy.

Throughout this time, Tom's goal wasn't to master each role but to figure out his strengths and interests. His development path was less about moving vertically and more about moving laterally to build a well-rounded understanding of the marketing ecosystem. With each new role, Tom gained a clearer picture of where he wanted to focus his energy long term. This spiral approach to development gave him a solid foundation and set him up for future success when he was ready to specialize and move up.

Here are several strategies you can adopt to support team members on a Spiral development path:

1. **Rotate through roles:** Facilitate rotations through different roles or projects within the same department, providing opportunities to experience various aspects of the business.

2. **Encourage cross-functional collaboration:** Support employees in joining cross-functional teams on projects where they can work with different departments and broaden their insights.

3. **Offer temporary rotations:** Provide short-term assignments or temporary roles in other functions to help employees gain exposure to different areas of the business.

4. **Arrange job shadowing:** Set up opportunities for employees to shadow colleagues in different departments or roles, giving them firsthand experience in various functions.

5. **Promote lateral moves:** Support lateral career moves that allow employees to gain experience in new roles or departments. These moves can be invaluable for those seeking to explore different functions and expand their horizons.

6. **Encourage reflective check-ins:** Regularly check in with employees to help them reflect on their experiences and identify areas where they feel most engaged. This can help them gain clarity on the direction they want to take.

By offering these opportunities, you enable employees to explore different roles and functions, helping them discover where their passions and strengths intersect. Spiral development isn't about going in circles—it's about gaining diverse experiences that ultimately guide them toward a fulfilling and impactful career.

Transitory Development

Transitory development is perhaps the most drastic form of growth, where an employee shifts across seemingly unrelated fields or disciplines. It's the path for those driven by a desire to explore new passions, take on fresh challenges, or pivot entirely into a different area of expertise. Unlike the linear or spiral paths, this development isn't just about progressing within a certain function—it's about making bold moves into new territories.

I've seen this development track firsthand with a client who transitioned from sales to human resources. They took their skills in relationship building and customer engagement and applied them in a completely different context, helping to shape company culture and employee experiences. My own journey mirrors this path as well—moving from the hospitality industry into leadership consulting. I made a significant leap, one motivated by a passion for exploring new ways to make an impact.

Employees on the Transitory development path often display a clear passion for areas outside their current role. They may actively engage in projects or conversations unrelated to their main job responsibilities, express a desire for significant change, or even feel unfulfilled in their current trajectory.

When I was at Hilton Hotels, for example, I found myself constantly wanting to design training, conduct workshops, and deliver presentations to other departments. In hindsight, I recognize that I was drawn to training and development. I was lucky that my manager, Marilyn, recognized my interest and energy for growing people. Instead of seeing it as a distraction from my role, she chose to support me. Marilyn gave me the time and space to develop workshops and deliver them to managers at other Hilton Hotels.

Even though I eventually left the company to open my consulting firm, during the time I was there, I was incredibly engaged because I was doing what I loved. I felt supported by my leader and the company and gave loads of discretionary effort as a result. That's the beauty of supporting transitory development—it's not only about where the employee might go in the future, but also about creating an environment where they feel valued and motivated to contribute at their highest level.

Leaders supporting transitory development can help facilitate these significant shifts by fostering an environment that values and encourages career experimentation. Here are some key strategies:

1. **Facilitate skill-building in a new discipline:** Provide opportunities for employees to explore and practice new skills.
2. **Make it safe:** Engage in open and honest conversations about aspirations, even if these shift away from their current jobs.
3. **Give time:** Provide opportunities to practice skills if possible.
4. **Encourage continuous learning:** Support employees seeking new skills in unrelated fields by providing access to training resources, workshops, and certifications that align with their new interests.
5. **Foster a culture of experimentation:** Create an environment where employees feel safe to explore new paths without fear of failure or retribution. Encourage them to share their interests and aspirations openly.
6. **Provide mentorship opportunities:** Connect employees with mentors who have successfully made similar transitions. These mentors can offer guidance, share their experiences, and help employees navigate the challenges of changing career paths.

By implementing these strategies, leaders can help employees on the Transitory development path successfully transition into new roles, fostering a culture of continuous learning, adaptability, and loyalty across the organization. Supporting these bold career moves not only benefits the individual but also enriches the team with diverse experiences and fresh perspectives.

Support Their Adventure

Those are the four types of development. Resist the urge to jump to conclusions about which one your employees want to pursue. The goal is to support them in their journey, whatever direction it takes. Observe and ask good questions to better understand their goals. Some questions I use to tease out a person's path include:

- What role or position in the company would you like to know more about?
- Are there different functions or areas within the organization you're curious about exploring? What attracts you to these areas?
- If you could learn one skill, what would it be? Why do you want to learn it?
- What other fields or roles outside of your current domain interest you?
- Are there any particular managerial or leadership skills you're interested in developing?
- What kind of professional growth opportunities would be ideal for you?
- How do you define success in your career path?
- Where do you see yourself in the next few years within our organization?
- If you could splurge on a conference, what would you choose?

Remember, interests change over time. What is true today may not be true tomorrow. In my twenties and thirties, linear development was very important to me. I wanted to grow and ascend the ranks in the hotel business because the positions and money were what interested me. Right now, I only want to grow my expertise.

Engage in these conversations every so often to make sure you are both on the same page, and that you're supporting your people the way they want and need to be supported.

Again, talent development is not an event; it happens all the time, especially in the Self-Awareness step. Sprinkle your regular interactions with opportunities for your people to reflect and gain self-intel. The more opportunities you create to build self-awareness for your employees, the easier and more efficient the process of developing your people becomes.

STEP TWO: OPPORTUNITIES

After laying the foundation of self-awareness, the next step in the development journey is aligning individual growth with the organization's needs. This is where personal development gains meaning—it connects the employee's aspirations to the company's mission and creates value for both. It's about showing how every skill, every new learning opportunity, contributes to our collective objectives.

To effectively navigate this step, the employee needs a solid understanding of the organizational strategy, team priorities, and goals, and must possess some business acumen to spot connections between the current and desired states. In other words, which areas make the most sense to develop in order to reach a future desired state? Once a baseline is established, the leader and team member can collaborate to seek opportunities to best develop toward where they want—or need—to be.

Guiding and mentoring employees requires two-way conversations, so it is beneficial to use an ask-directed approach here. Gently nudge the employee toward thinking about the business in a more holistic way, independently finding ways to create value:

- How do you think your job might change in the next two years, given the organizational strategy? Will this shift create any skill gaps? How can you acquire those skills?

- What are you doing more of now that you were not doing a year ago? Is that a trend? Do you need to learn more about it to better navigate this change? Can you think of any internal resources that might help with this?
- How do you see yourself supporting the team's new mandate? What do you need in order to do that?
- Given you want to move to a management position, how would you structure your learning path? What skill would you want to develop first? Why? How can you gain that skill?

The goal isn't to dictate what the employee needs to develop or how they should go about it, but to teach them how to assess and take charge of their own development.

If an employee proposes something seemingly unrelated to their current role, like a basket weaving course, probe deeper. Ask how this aligns with their aspirations or the company's strategy. If they can draw a meaningful connection, consider it. If not, suggest alternative opportunities that are more aligned with the company's goal and their own. Help them link their ideas to tangible results.

Setting aside dedicated time for more structured conversations about opportunities, perhaps on a quarterly basis, is helpful. These one-on-ones connect the dots between the ongoing self-awareness dialogue and the broader development path, ensuring that both leader and employee are aligned and moving forward together.

Now, what if the employee doesn't want to explore opportunities? What if they think they are at the point in their career they don't need to develop? Well, development is not an option.

You may have seasoned professionals who prefer the familiar tools and methods that have served them well rather than adopting new technologies. This resistance to change, while understandable, can hinder not only their own journey but also the team's progress. One of my clients, in a senior role, refuses to use Slack, sticking to email or text. He claims this is because he has enough on his plate, but the real issue is reluctance to learn a new skill. His team has to do extra work to loop him into conversations, slowing down collaboration and creating bottlenecks. He's often not informed about real-time developments and, as a result, makes decisions without the full context. Without clear expectations from his leader about the importance of embracing new tools, this employee sees no reason to evolve his way of working.

In today's fast-paced world, standing still means falling behind. We are all walking up an escalator, except the escalator is going down. At best, we can get a step or two ahead, but if we stop, we move backward. Growing skills is not optional, and development isn't just future-focused; it's enabling performance today.

Let's look at an example of how aligning employee aspirations with organizational needs can play out in practice.

Meet Katrina, a team leader in a midsized software development company dedicated to building her team's talents through ongoing awareness discussions. Carlos, a standout software developer on her team, recently expressed interest in deepening his expertise in emerging technologies, specifically in artificial intelligence (AI) and machine learning (ML), areas that the company is looking to expand into.

Katrina sees a valuable opportunity for Carlos to align his career aspirations with the strategic direction of the company. The industry's rapid growth in AI and ML presents a perfect canvas for Carlos to carve out a niche for himself while contributing significantly to the company's innovative edge.

Katrina schedules a focused one-on-one meeting with Carols to discuss potential pathways for him to engage more deeply with AI and ML projects, leveraging the groundwork laid by their previous conversations.

Katrina: (Opening the meeting with a positive tone) Carlos, our talks about your interest in AI and ML have really stayed with me. I believe there's a golden opportunity here for you and for us as a company. How do you feel about diving deeper into this area?

Carlos: (Showing enthusiasm) I've been really excited about the prospect, Katrina. I've started to do some self-study, but I'm not exactly sure how to make a significant shift toward working on AI and ML projects here.

Katrina: I'm glad you're taking the initiative. Given our company's push toward integrating more AI and ML into our projects, your timing couldn't be better. We need to build our capacity in these areas, and your technical foundation gives you a head start. What specific aspects of AI and ML are you most drawn to?

Carlos: I'm particularly fascinated by natural language processing and its applications. I see a lot of potential for us to incorporate NLP into our customer service solutions.

Katrina: NLP is a fantastic focus area and highly relevant to our goals. Let's think about how we can develop your expertise further. There are several online courses and certifications in NLP that could be beneficial. Also, we have some upcoming projects where you could get hands-on experience. How does that align with your thoughts?

Carlos: That aligns perfectly. As I mentioned before, I'm already looking at some courses but wasn't sure which ones would be most useful. And getting practical experience on projects sounds like exactly what I need.

Katrina: Great! How about we outline a plan where you start with a foundational course in NLP, and then we gradually involve you in relevant projects as you build your knowledge? We can also look for opportunities for you to collaborate with our current AI specialists. This way, you get to learn from their experience while applying your skills in real-world scenarios.

Carlos: That sounds like a solid plan. I appreciate the guidance and the opportunity to grow in this direction. What's our first step?

Katrina: Why don't you research courses and set a timeline for potential completion, and then we'll review how we get you involved in the upcoming AI project. Let's catch up again in two weeks to discuss your progress and any new insights you might have.

Carlos: Sounds good, Katrina. I'm eager to get started. Thanks for supporting me in this journey.

Katrina: Absolutely, Carlos. It's exciting to see your enthusiasm. Remember, this is a journey we're on together. I'm here to support you every step of the way.

This step is about identifying opportunities that match personal interests with team or organizational needs. By guiding your team members through this process, you help them see how growth not only benefits their own careers, but also contributes to the broader success of the organization, creating a win-win for both the individual and the company.

STEP THREE: GOALS

After exploring and identifying the right growth opportunities, the next step is to set goals that provide clarity and define success for the desired outcome.

Your direct report has, through good self-analysis, landed on an aspiration to move into a supervisory role. This aligns well with a greater team objective as you would like someone to take on some of your tasks, giving you time to be more strategic and future-focused. Now it's time for them to write down the goal, with your support, so they have clarity and focus.

If your organization has a personal development plan (PDP) process, use it. If not, create your own simple process. You can use SMART criteria or the OKRs framework, whatever is easier and makes sense for your team. If needed, teach your employees a framework and encourage them to use it to capture and develop the goals.

For the employee aspiring to move into a supervisory role, their SMART goals might look like this:

Specific: Transition into a supervisory role within the team.

Measurable: Lead a project team to achieve a specific project milestone, improving team productivity by 20 percent within the next six months.

Achievable: Take a foundational leadership training program, participate in the company mentorship program, and lead a small team project as a trial.

Relevant: Step into a supervisory role, which is a career aspiration; for the team, cultivate internal leadership to drive team performance.

Time-bound: Complete leadership training and mentorship within three months, followed by leading a project team to achieve its goal in the subsequent three months; secure a supervisory role within one year.

If you use the OKR framework, the employee's goals might look like this:

Objective: Secure and excel in a supervisory role within the next twelve months.

KR1: Complete a foundational leadership training program and participate in at least three sessions with a mentor supervisor by the end of quarter two.

KR2: Lead a pilot project team, applying learned leadership skills to improve team productivity by 20 percent.

No matter the framework you choose, the key is to ensure the employee creates a specific goal that is both meaningful and aligned with the organization's broader objectives. In the process of guiding your team members through this process, you're building accountability and ownership.

STEP FOUR: PLANNING

A goal without a plan is just a wish—we've heard this many times. So true. If the goal is well structured, as with the SMART or OKRs, tying it to a plan is not difficult. Again, this is the employee's responsibility, but you can help and guide the process. Sometimes your employee will need direction or time to research and learn what the path to attaining the goal entails.

Encourage the employee to take each Achievable or KR and build it out with dates and dependencies. For example:

Objective: Transition into a supervisory role within the team, focusing on enhancing team productivity and engagement.

Step 1: Complete Leadership Training (Months One Through Three)

- Action: Enroll in a foundational leadership training program.
- Objective: Build essential leadership skills, including communication, conflict resolution, and team management.
- Milestone: Complete the training program by the end of the third month.
- Check-in: Schedule regular discussions with manager to review progress and apply key learnings to your current role.

Step 2: Participate in the Mentorship Program (Months One Through Six)

- Action: Join the company's mentorship program and connect with a senior leader or supervisor.
- Objective: Gain insights into leadership responsibilities, decision-making, and team dynamics.
- Milestone: Participate in at least three mentorship sessions in the first three months and continue with regular sessions for the next three months.
- Check-in: Reflect with the mentor on leadership experi-

ences and gather feedback on your readiness for supervisory tasks.

Step 3: Lead a Small Team Project (Months Four Through Six)

- Action: Take responsibility for a small team project as a trial run for a supervisory role.
- Objective: Apply leadership training and mentorship learnings in a real-world setting by managing a team to complete a project milestone.
- Milestone: Successfully lead the team to achieve a key project objective, with a focus on improving team productivity by 20 percent.
- Check-in: After the project, gather feedback from both the team and your manager on your leadership performance.

Step 4: Reflect and Adjust (Months Six Through Seven)

- Action: Take time to reflect on the leadership experience and feedback from the first project.
- Objective: Identify areas of strength and opportunities for improvement.
- Milestone: Adjust approach for future leadership roles based on feedback.
- Check-in: Discuss with manager and mentor how to continue to grow and develop for future projects.

Step 5: Lead a Larger or More Complex Project (Months Seven Through Ten)

- Action: Take on a more complex project or lead a larger team.

- Objective: Demonstrate increased leadership ability by managing a more significant initiative and driving team performance.
- Milestone: Achieve the project's goals, ensuring team productivity and engagement are sustained or improved.
- Check-in: Have a midyear performance review with manager to assess readiness for a formal supervisory role.

Step 6: Secure a Supervisory Role (Months Eleven Through Twelve)

- Action: Apply for or be formally considered for a supervisory role within the team.
- Objective: Use leadership training, mentorship, and hands-on project management experience to transition into the supervisory role.
- Milestone: Successfully transition into a supervisory role by the end of the twelve-month period.
- Check-in: Once in the role, continue working with mentor and manager to set new leadership development goals for career growth.

Yes, this plan might seem arduous, but don't you plan for every project? And this project of employee development might be your most important one! A well-defined plan outlines the specific actions, timelines, and resources needed to achieve development goals. It ensures both the leader and employee stay aligned and accountable, creating a road map for progress and success.

STEP FIVE: DEPENDENCIES

In the context of career development, "dependencies" refer to the factors outside an employee's direct control that are necessary for them to achieve their goals. This could involve the support of others, access to resources, or external conditions that influence their progress. As a leader, your role is to help identify these dependencies and assist your employee in overcoming any obstacles by providing guidance, resources, or connections.

Let's face it: who you know matters. One of the most important dependencies is building connections—both within and outside the organization. Employees may need introductions to key stakeholders, mentors, or cross-functional teams that can offer new opportunities or provide valuable feedback. Encourage your direct report to network with people who can offer insights or open doors to new projects, roles, or mentorships.

When we talk about opening doors, we're referring to providing opportunities that the employee might not have direct access to. For example, you can help facilitate introductions to senior leaders, recommend them for stretch assignments, or advocate for their participation in key projects that align with their career goals. This type of support is crucial for helping employees gain visibility and access to development opportunities that might otherwise be out of reach.

As a leader, you can also provide support in several key areas:

- **Access to resources:** Ensure your employee has access to the tools, training, and information they need to succeed in their development plan.
- **Mentorship and sponsorship:** Either mentor the employee directly or connect them with a more experienced leader who can provide additional guidance and support.

- **Advocacy:** Act as a sponsor within the organization by advocating for your employee in meetings, recommending them for new roles or projects, and ensuring their contributions are recognized.
- **Guidance on obstacles:** Help your employee identify potential obstacles or challenges in their plan and work with them to develop strategies to overcome these roadblocks.

Finally, it's critical to review the goals and plan collaboratively, ensuring both of you are clear on where support is needed. This sets the stage for clear next steps and holds both the employee and you, as the leader, accountable for ensuring progress is made.

TALENT DEVELOPMENT SUMMARY

This chapter emphasizes the critical role of leaders in guiding the growth and development of their teams. It stresses that talent development is a shared responsibility between the employee, the organization, and the leader. Leaders should focus on continuous learning and development, not just for immediate performance, but to build long-term agility, innovation, and leadership within their teams. The chapter also explores four development paths—Linear, Expert, Spiral, and Transitory—and offers a structured approach to career development through self-awareness, goal setting, and planning.

Why Is Development Important?

Growth and development is one of the most sought after benefits employees look for, and it is equally important for organizations because it:

- **Drives engagement and retention:** Employees who grow in their roles are more engaged and committed to the organization.
- **Fosters agility and change:** A broader skill set helps teams quickly adapt to market demands and organizational shifts.
- **Prompts innovation and creativity:** Exposure to new experiences pushes employees to think beyond routine and find creative solutions.
- **Prepares future leaders:** Developing talent today ensures a strong leadership pipeline for the future, safeguarding organizational knowledge.

When to Develop Talent

Although development is an ongoing endeavor, there are certain situations when it comes to the forefront:

- Always...Yes, talent development is always a key part of what a leader does. You don't perform this task alone, but you are a part of the process.
- When employee responsibilities shift.
- When employees need a new challenge.
- When new skills are needed.
- When the employee has expressed interest in development.

How to Develop Talent

Here are some of the most effective methods covered in this chapter for kickstarting the development process from a leader's perspective:

- Discuss aspirations, desires, motivators, and interests.
- Clarify skill gaps and future needs with the individual.
- Link aspirations with organizational strategy whenever possible.

- Allow people to try new ways of doing things.
- Collaboratively create a development plan that will build capacity, skills, and engagement.
- Encourage your employees to find growth opportunities themselves.

YOUR CHALLENGE

Ready for another challenge? Reflect on what it means for you to embrace the growth and development of people as your highest calling as a leader. How does this resonate with your personal leadership philosophy and the legacy you want to create?

I've been there, sitting across from someone with untapped potential, knowing that with the right support, they could soar. It's a pretty incredible feeling, right? But here's the thing: it's not just about seeing potential—it's about taking action to nurture it.

So here's my challenge to you: think about your own leadership journey. Who helped you get to where you are today? Now, how can you pay that forward to your team?

Find two people who are ready to grow, and schedule one-on-one meetings with them. Share the roles and responsibilities of development and discuss their career aspirations, strengths, and development areas. Use open-ended questions to guide these conversations, focusing on understanding their professional goals and how they align with the team's objectives.

Based on the insights gained from these discussions, work together with each team member to draft a personalized development plan. This plan should include specific goals, action steps, and milestones. Ensure these plans are flexible enough to evolve over time.

Support your people in implementing the development plans. This might involve providing resources, assigning mentorship roles, facilitating training opportunities, or reallocating work to provide new challenges. Regularly check in on progress and adjust the plans as necessary.

Reflect on how you can foster an environment that values continuous growth and development. Implement at least one change in your team's culture that encourages open dialogue about career aspirations, celebrates learning achievements, and supports taking on new challenges.

The ultimate goal of this challenge is to integrate talent development into the DNA of your leadership style and your team's culture. By actively engaging in these steps, you are not only contributing to the growth of your team members but also building a legacy of leadership that prioritizes and values development.

A thriving environment of growth and development leads to the one thing that can take a team to the next level and turn it into something greater than the sum of its parts—collaboration.

Chapter Seven

CULTIVATE COLLABORATION

"Not finance. Not strategy. Not technology. It is teamwork that remains the ultimate competitive advantage, both because it is so powerful and so rare."

—PATRICK LENCIONI

In 2019, a moment in scientific history captivated the world: the unveiling of the first-ever image of a black hole. This achievement wasn't the work of a single individual, organization, or even a single country. It resulted from years of relentless collaboration across the globe, involving over two hundred researchers from different countries, institutions, and areas of expertise. The Event Horizon Telescope project connected a network of eight preexisting telescopes across the planet, effectively creating a planet-sized observatory capable of capturing an image of the elusive black hole located in the M87 galaxy, fifty-five million light-years away.

I need to be honest: I'm not really into astrology. But as the world admired the images, I was mesmerized by the idea that so many people synchronized their efforts—from the South Pole to the Sierra Nevada mountains, and from the peaks of Hawaii to the deserts of Chile, across different time zones, languages, and cultures. This effort required not only technological innovation and coordination, but a shared commitment to a common goal that was so important it transcended individual aspirations or national pride.

If scientists from around the world can work in sync across continents to capture the unseen, why do leaders struggle to cultivate collaborations among team members just a few steps away from each other?

Collaboration has always been a cornerstone of successful teams and organizations. As Patrick Lencioni states, it is the ultimate competitive advantage. This is more true now than ever as work has become more complex, involving intricate projects that span various disciplines and geographies and cross-functional teams operating within agile frameworks. The pace at which decisions need to be made and executed has accelerated, so teams need to share knowledge quickly and adapt to rapid technological advancements. The competitive landscape is driving the need for constant innovation, which thrives in collaborative environments, but creating that environment is usually a challenge for leaders. Since the pandemic, I have spent more time helping teams build stronger collaboration than in the previous fifteen years collectively. This reflects the need and dedication of leaders to enable their teams to optimize their performance and leverage the power of collaboration.

From the vast outer space to the conference rooms of our offices or our dining rooms, we need strategies to build a strong collaborative culture in our teams and organizations.

COLLABORATION DEFINED

As Confucius said, "The beginning of wisdom is to call things by their proper name." So, let's clearly define what we mean by "collaboration."

First, let me get this out of the way: regular team meetings, standups, updates, and huddles are *not* collaborations. They are important, they provide opportunities for dialogue and connection, and they need to happen, but let's not muddy the waters and call them collaborations.

In its purest form, collaboration is an act of working with another person or group of people to create or produce something of value. Simple, to the point, and intuitive. But doing that work is not easy. Why is that?

Collaboration isn't just about people working together; it's a dynamic process where diverse individuals combine their expertise and share their ideas, resources, and efforts to find opportunities, solve problems, and create value beyond achieving goals. It's the diversity of experiences, opinions, and knowledge that make collaboration simultaneously challenging and productive. If a like-minded group of people come together to solve a problem, they could easily Band-Aid the problem instead of pushing the boundaries and innovating. In situations where a single person cannot solve the problem alone, collaboration comes to the rescue. As teams work together, they not only find solutions but often innovate in unexpected ways.

Working together involves a complex system of synergy and integration of skills that requires focus, intention, leadership, and tension—yes, even conflict. Leaders today recognize that the success of their team and organization hinges on good teamwork. The problem is that they don't know how to optimize it.

COLLABORATION CHALLENGES

Let's explore some common collaboration challenges and how they play out in the real world. Are your teams experiencing any of these?

Take a team at an emerging digital art platform company, ArtFusion, working on integrating a new feature that uses artificial intelligence to recommend personalized art projects to its users. The team includes AI developers, user interface designers, digital artists, and marketing professionals, each bringing unique perspectives from different cultural and professional backgrounds. As we explore their journey, think about what challenges your team is facing that may be getting in the way of effective collaboration.

Challenge 1: Virtual and Hybrid Dynamics. In remote and hybrid work environments, collaboration challenges are more pronounced. Time zone differences, limited face-to-face interaction, and reliance on digital tools can reduce the quality of communication and slow down progress.

At ArtFusion, the geographical spread of the team had an impact on a product launch date schedule. With AI developers in Eastern Europe and marketing professionals in Silicon Valley, the time zone gap caused delays, pushing crucial decisions to the following day. As a result, the team struggled to finalize decisions on the AI-powered feature, ultimately pushing the launch date back by a few weeks.

Challenge 2: Unclear Vision. A shared vision is essential for any team to succeed, but when the direction isn't clear, team members can easily drift into conflicting priorities. Without a strong, unified understanding of the project's goals, teams may find themselves working at cross-purposes, leading to confusion, frustration, and wasted effort.

The team at ArtFusion lacked a unifying vision. They were

passionate about the product, but each member saw it from their own perspective. While the AI developers focused on creating a cutting-edge algorithm, the UX designers pushed for a simple and intuitive user experience, leading to competing priorities. As marketing added new requirements to match industry trends, the team found themselves constantly revisiting the project's milestones, resulting in scope creep and inefficiencies that slowed progress.

Challenge 3: Complexity in Diversity. While diversity in skills and perspectives is a key driver of innovation, it can also present significant challenges in terms of decision-making and alignment. Teams with diverse expertise can have different priorities, making it difficult to agree on solutions. Inclusive leadership can harness these differences productively, avoiding gridlock.

The ArtFusion team faced this challenge as AI specialists, predominantly from Eastern Europe, prioritized sophisticated algorithms that predicted user needs with high accuracy but required complex user inputs. In contrast, the user experience designers from North America wanted simplicity and minimal user interaction to ensure accessibility and ease of use. These differing approaches caused tension in meetings, as each team advocated for their own position.

Challenge 4: Ambiguous Measurement. Measuring the team's health, an indicator of how a team is performing, is a difficult task. The traditional metrics, like customer satisfaction and feature adoption rates, don't show the collaborative health of the team during the product development phase. Similarly, regular sprint reviews conducted to assess progress focus on immediate deliverables without providing insights into ongoing collaborative dynamics or long-term project sustainability. This ambiguity in measurement leads to challenges in understanding true project success and can mask underlying issues in team collaboration and integration.

At ArtFusion, sprint reviews and deliverables were the primary focus. However, the team members' inner-working issues—especially between the AI and UX teams—went unnoticed. The lack of insight into the team's collaborative health meant that unresolved tensions and miscommunications were allowed to build up, ultimately threatening the success of the AI-powered feature.

Challenge 5: Low Trust and High Tension. Trust is the foundation of effective collaboration. When trust is low, tensions often run high, leading to strained communication, defensive behavior, a reluctance to share ideas openly, and difficulty resolving conflicts, which leads to delays in progress and a breakdown in overall cohesion. Without trust, every disagreement feels like a threat, rather than an opportunity to problem-solve together.

At ArtFusion, this breakdown in trust came to a head during a critical feature handoff. The engineering team was ready to implement the AI-driven recommendation engine, but marketing made last-minute changes to the feature's user-facing components, driven by a competitor's release. Engineers, feeling blindsided, pushed back on the new requirements, claiming they would compromise the stability of the system. Marketing, meanwhile, was adamant that the changes were necessary to stay relevant. The lack of trust between the teams caused a complete standstill, as neither side was willing to compromise. Deadlines passed while both departments remained locked in a stalemate, unable to move forward until leadership intervened to mediate a solution.

Challenge 6: Resource Allocation. Limited resources— whether time, budget, or personnel—can strain team dynamics, leading to decreased productivity and increased stress. Teams forced to juggle competing priorities often find it difficult to stay focused, which ultimately affects the quality of their work and collaboration.

ArtFusion faced significant challenges when the AI team was reassigned to another high-priority project. This left the UX designers without the necessary engineering support, stalling their progress and further weakening the team's ability to collaborate effectively under pressure.

Challenge 7: Change Resistance. Collaboration inherently involves change. When teams are asked to adopt new processes, technologies, or strategies, resistance often follows. Whether it's due to comfort with familiar methods or fear of the unknown, this resistance can slow down progress and create friction within the team.

Given their geographical distribution, each individual ArtFusion team had their own preferred project management tools. When the whole group was asked to adopt one tool that would be consistent across all departments, they spent time trying to "sell" each other on the advantages of their familiar methods. It took the team a while to finally align on using the same tool, losing valuable productive time in the process.

Challenge 8: Unproductive Meetings. Meetings are meant to drive progress. Let me say that again: meetings are meant to drive progress. But when they lack engagement or structure, they can quickly become unproductive. Whether it's low participation, avoiding uncomfortable topics, or unclear agendas, unproductive meetings not only waste time but also weaken team morale and stifle creativity. Teams can leave feeling more disconnected, with little resolution on key issues.

In the case of ArtFusion, virtual meetings often fell flat. Many team members kept their cameras off, and discussions lacked engagement. Important topics, such as missed deadlines and unclear responsibilities, were often skirted to avoid conflict. As a result, meetings became checkboxes rather than opportunities to address core challenges. This lack of meaningful interaction meant that team members left meetings feeling no closer to solutions than when they started.

Do any of these challenges resonate?

These challenges often bleed into one another, requiring the leader to take proactive steps to understand the core issue and work at bridging these divides, fostering an environment where diverse talents are leveraged constructively and where a strong culture of collaboration is continuously cultivated.

In the following sections, we will explore strategies for optimizing and effectively addressing these challenges and ensuring that collaboration is productive and leads to successful outcomes.

TEAMS THAT PERFORM

During one of my regular coaching sessions, a client, a VP of Sales at a large company, expressed feelings of extreme exhaustion. To be honest, it's not uncommon for my clients to feel that these days, but in her case, it felt different. The fatigue was palpable. She shared that her team of directors was not working well together. They escalated most issues to her and struggled to make decisions and resolve problems amongst themselves. She was out of bandwidth, and she noticed that the situation was getting worse.

I probed for some background information to better understand the dynamics at play. Her department had recently undergone a significant transformation. A new director was hired, and the team was restructured to better meet the needs of the market. The entire team consisted of about seventy people, led by eight directors, with my client at the helm.

The senior leadership team had a clear mandate: to get revenues on track for the rest of the year. The sales team was resourced right, and it was time to hit the ground running. To succeed, they needed to work well together across different functions, capitalizing on their talents, experience, and client relationships. But in order for the sales team to coalesce, the directors needed to agree on a unified vision, identify priorities, build trust, and begin functioning as one unit. Doing so would not only provide direction their teams needed but role model good collaboration.

After listening and assessing the situation, I realized my client's team was in the "Storming" phase of the team development curve identified by Bruce Tuckman in his 1965 Team Development Model. While some may see it as outdated, this model has seen a resurgence in recent years because of its timeless value. It remains highly relevant because it taps into fundamental human dynamics that persist regardless of industry, role, or time period.

I use this model with clients because it is a simple but powerful tool for leaders to gain **situational awareness**—one of the pillars of Intentional Leadership. By understanding where their team is in the development process, they can avoid frustration and instead guide their team through the natural phases of growth-intentional action. The model also emphasizes the importance of **self-awareness**, recognizing how the leader's own actions and style impact the team's development.

By applying this model with an Intentional Leadership mindset, you can unlock a deeper understanding of how your team is evolving and take the **intentional action** to accelerate progress, overcome obstacles, and ultimately build a high-performing group that not only focuses on individual contributions but also truly collaborates to achieve collective success.

Team Development Curve

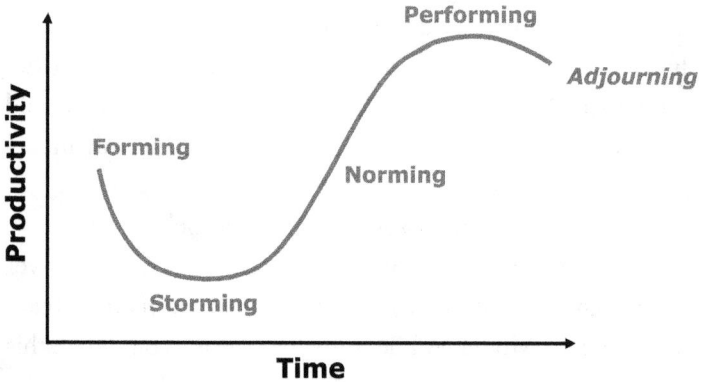

Adapted from Bruce W. Tuckman's Team Development Model (1965)

Before we go into the phases, let me say a few things about this model that are often not mentioned.

- For a team to reach its optimum performance, it must go through each phase. There is no skipping steps. It's work, yes, sometimes hard work. But the system cannot be hacked.
- For true collaboration to happen, the team must be in the Performing phase. You're fooling yourself if you think that the team is at full potential if they are anywhere else on the curve.
- During the Forming and Storming phases, the team members function as individuals working in their silos.
- The Forming and Storming phases are very import-

ant. Teams that stay too long in Performing enter what is sometimes referred to as the Adjourning or Mourning phase, which sees a decline in performance. Actively cycling through each phase ensures that the team remains dynamic, relevant, and continuously delivering value.

- Most teams believe they are in Norming and Performing—ironic because 99 percent of the time I am brought in to help a team get unstuck. I always want to say, "Is me being here not a clue that things are not the best?"
- The leader has a huge influence on how quickly the team transitions through the curve.

Let's explore each phase, your role, and practical strategies for moving your team through.

FORMING

This initial stage of team development is crucial as members come together to learn about the team's purpose and each other's roles. I have this vivid memory of my son Tim, who, at the age of five, went to his first soccer practice—being Polish, that sport is part of our DNA.

It was a beautiful sunny day. Imagine the excited kids on the green field running around in oversized shorts. The coach threw the ball onto the field, and the kids swarmed it, chasing it in whatever direction it was rolling. At one point a plane flew across the sky, and the kids stopped playing and momentarily stared at the plane before continuing to chase the ball without purpose.

As with my son and his teammates, teams in the Forming stage experience initial excitement, which creates energy and some movement toward the goal, often by accident. The performance, however, is not sustainable as the desired outcomes are not yet clearly defined, and the team members are easily distracted, lacking priorities and focus. The graph shows that the productivity axis peaks slightly in this initial phase.

How do you know if your team is Forming? Obviously, when a new team is assembled. Established teams move into Forming when they experience significant changes, such as new members joining, shifts in roles, or a strategic pivot—any of which can have a huge impact, like changing the rules of a soccer game.

At this point, the leader plays a central role, setting the foundation for the team's future dynamics and success. Here is what team members need in the Forming phase.

Clarity

Define the team's purpose and vision. Remember the magic of a vision we explored in Chapter Three? Members need to understand and be able to articulate why the team exists, what they are solving for, and how they will get there. Communicate key messages seven times—yes, seven! Of course, use different modes to ensure the messages are heard and absorbed.

Expectations

Provide clear guidance by setting goals and establishing processes. This creates focus and identifies priorities, especially during the early stages when confusion can easily derail progress.

For instance, maybe you want the team to focus more on the effort than the result; that would probably be the case in our kids' soccer example. By setting clear expectations—like making precision passing the top priority—the coach ensures the team doesn't only focus on scoring goals, but learns how to best work together and capitalize on each other's talents.

As we explored in Chapter Four, the clearer your expectations are, the more room you give your team to focus on the work itself—because they're not spending energy trying to figure out what you want.

Rules

Set some basic guidelines for behavior, communication, and processes right from the start. These initial ground rules help you avoid those awkward moments when everyone's wondering, "Can I say that?" or "Should I have sent that email in ALL CAPS?"

As the team matures, they'll refine and define their own norms, but early on, they need these guardrails to guide their interactions. Keep it simple—as with expectations, there's no need to overwhelm the team with too many rules. Start with two or three. Some of the teams I work with begin with just one, like, "Assume positive intent." You know your team best. Choose norms that fit your team's needs and the culture you want to create.

Here are a few examples from my clients:

- **Seek to understand first:** before jumping to conclusions, take a beat and listen.
- **Stay curious:** encourage asking questions, even if it feels uncomfortable.
- **No wrong ideas:** create a safe space where team members aren't afraid to throw out wild ideas.
- **Own your stuff:** be accountable for your actions and decisions, no finger-pointing.

- **Share early, share often:** avoid holding onto information until it's too late to act.

The norms you establish in Forming set the stage for open, respectful interactions. Think of them as training wheels guiding your team until they build their own rules of engagement as they grow through the development curve.

Connection

During this phase, interactions among team members tend to be polite and superficial as they explore the boundaries of their tasks and relationships. Create opportunities for team members to build relationships and establish trust. It's really hard to be honest and vulnerable in the absence of trust.

Allocate time for team members to get to know each other. Use tools like DiSC, Working Genius, or other fun activities, like trivia, to explore the team's unique strengths, communication styles, and areas where they differ and complement one another. If you dive straight into productive work, the team may find it difficult to become anything more than a group of individuals. And the next phase, Storming, can be hell!

Support

Your team is embarking on a new journey, and as their leader, it's important to be there as a steady guidepost. Be proactive in offering your support by addressing uncertainties and issues as they arise. At this early stage, team members are likely navigating new relationships, roles, and responsibilities, which can feel overwhelming. Ensure that you're available to provide clarity and reassurance, whether that's through one-on-one conversations, team check-ins, or being responsive when questions come up.

Anticipate potential stumbling blocks—whether logistical, interpersonal, or project-related—and step in before they become real problems. Support at this stage is less about solving every issue and more about creating a sense of security for the team as they get to know the landscape. When people know that you've got their back, they're more likely to take risks, ask for help, and collaborate with confidence.

Without a doubt, the Forming stage is one of the trickiest for any leader. It demands patience, time, and way more communication than you probably thought possible—sometimes repetitive to the point where you could swear you've said the same thing twenty times. It may feel like you're running a personal TED Talk on loop. But hang in there! All that groundwork is what helps your team find their groove, build trust, and gain momentum. Remember: go slow to go fast. In the Performing stage, the team will be self-reliant, collaborate at its highest level, and will forget you exist!

Being proactive in the Forming stage can save time and prevent dysfunctions from surfacing later in Storming.

A TOOL TO AID TEAM DEVELOPMENT

As we wrap up the discussion on the Forming stage, I want to share a resource I often use to help teams navigate this tricky phase: *The Five Dysfunctions of a Team* by Patrick Lencioni. The premise of the model is that in order for a team to achieve its optimum performance, it needs to work through five behaviors identified as key barriers or dysfunctions that impact a team's success: lack of trust, fear of conflict, lack of commitment, avoidance of accountability, and inattention to results. The framework is represented as a pyramid with trust at the base.

- **Trust:** This is the foundation for any effective team, where members feel safe to express ideas, admit mistakes, and be vulnerable without fear of judgment.
- **Conflict:** Once trust is built, teams can engage in open, constructive discussions, expressing diverse viewpoints that lead to innovation and better decision-making.
- **Commitment:** After working through conflict, the team achieves clarity and buy-in from all members, ensuring alignment and dedication to shared goals.
- **Accountability:** With commitment comes accountability, as team members hold each other to high standards and ensure everyone is contributing effectively.

- **Results:** All of this leads to a focus on collective success, with teams prioritizing shared outcomes over individual or departmental ambitions.

If you think this framework would be helpful for your team, I recommend getting Patrick Lencioni's book. It outlines practical strategies for overcoming each dysfunction. If you're looking for a more data-driven approach, there is a comprehensive assessment that teams can take to evaluate how they rate in each of the five behaviors. The results provide objective insights into a team's strengths and areas for improvement, offering a great benchmark for understanding what might be getting in the way of effective collaboration and high performance.

STORMING

This phase is when I usually get the call for help! Storming isn't where you take out your umbrellas; it's where you learn to dance in the rain.

Why does this stage happen? Well, team members are beginning to express their opinions, test boundaries, and vie for influence as they start to feel comfortable within the group. The initial "honeymoon" of Forming wears off, and the team begins to encounter real differences in ideas, communication styles, and approaches to work. This is a natural and important part of team growth. Conflict, while uncomfortable, is necessary because it forces the team to address underlying issues, align on goals, and establish the norms that will allow them to move forward as a cohesive unit. Teams that don't go through this phase properly tend to stagnate, operating under the illusion of harmony, when in reality, unresolved tensions are just bubbling beneath the surface.

While disruptive, uncomfortable, and generally gross, this phase is normal and crucial for the development of a strong and healthy team. Unfortunately, some teams get stuck in Storming for a long time, building resentment and scarring that sometimes takes time to undo so the team is set on the right course.

Going back to the situation the VP of Sales described—what she was experiencing was classic Storming behaviors. As is typical in this phase, team members struggled to work together. The trust had not been built yet, and roles and responsibilities were unclear, due to the recent reorganization and the arrival of a new director. Common approaches to communication and problem-solving had not been established, which resulted in higher dependency on my client to handle escalations and resolve tensions. This was a pivotal moment for her to step in and actively guide her team through this developmental stage.

Here's what teams need during Storming.

Patience

Give time and space for your team and yourself to breathe. This phase is messy and time-consuming. Resist the urge to resolve conflicts quickly and move on, as rushing through Storming only leads to superficial fixes. Let your team debate, discuss, and yes, disagree. Give them room to work through tensions so they can arrive at meaningful solutions. Trust that this slower pace will pay off in stronger, long-term collaboration.

Exercising patience can be very hard! I often have to battle with myself not to speak up and solve. Anything longer than three seconds of dead air makes me cringe. But I've learned to manage my self-talk, and now I see that the best outcomes come after some silence.

Communication

Open, honest, and frequent communication is key to getting through the Storming phase. Encourage your team to raise concerns directly, but make sure they do it respectfully.

To start the conversation, I love to ask this question: "What do we need to talk about that we don't?" Or if that's too direct, I might say, "I sense frustration. Am I picking up on that correctly?"

If the team is deep in Storming, they might be hesitant to speak up. When I see this, I reinforce with the team how important it is to address issues that might get in the way of achieving the team's vision or purpose. Unspoken frustrations bubble up and cause bigger issues down the road, so guide your team in building the confidence to address problems before they explode.

Prompt meta-thinking to help the team to reflect not only on what they're working on, but how they're working together. Ask, "How do you feel this discussion is going?" or "What's working well in our communication, and what could we improve?" These questions nudge the team to step back, spot patterns, and make adjustments that strengthen collaboration. It's like giving them the mirror they didn't know they needed—helping them see how to improve without you doing all the heavy lifting.

Psychological Safety

The discomfort of Storming can only be mitigated if team members feel safe expressing themselves. Psychological safety is the belief that you won't be punished or humiliated for speaking up with ideas, questions, and concerns, or when you make a mistake. Fostering psychological safety among your team or department is massively important. It builds confidence among team members that their peers' intentions are good and that there is no reason to be protective or careful around the group. In essence, psychological safety boils down to trust. When trust exists, teammates can get used to being vulnerable with one another.

How do leaders promote psychological safety? Take intentional time away from discussing tasks to focus on the people behind the work. Whether it's quarterly, monthly, or even weekly, create space for sharing and connecting on a human level, apart from deadlines, numbers, and results. At the beginning of meetings, especially virtual ones, conduct quick activities that get your team members sharing, learning about each other, and building bonds. Simple exercises include "Rose, Bud, Thorn"—best part of their week (Rose), biggest frustration (Thorn), and something learned (Bud)—or Happiest/Proudest and Saddest/Angriest moments of the week.

You can't expect your people to be vulnerable if you aren't willing to do the same. Leaders need to model vulnerability and humility—showing that you, too, are human. Admit when you don't have all the answers, or when you've made a mistake. Your transparency paves the way for your team to follow suit.

Lastly, be mindful of how you respond to your team. Leaders set the tone. Are your responses encouraging, or do you accidentally embarrass people? My life mantra: *Be soft on people, and hard on the issue.* For example, if someone on your team misses a deadline, saying, "You didn't meet the deadline," is hard on the person and doesn't address the real issue. Instead, try something like, "I know you've been under a lot of pressure—what can I do to support you so we can meet this deadline next time?" This approach acknowledges the issue without judgment and focuses on empowering the person to succeed moving forward.

You'll know you've reached a place of psychological safety when people openly contribute, offer differing opinions, and aren't afraid to admit when they're wrong. That's when collaboration can truly thrive.

PSYCHOLOGICAL SAFETY AT WORK

In late 2023, Wiley published new research centered on whether or not people feel safe to take a risk in their organizations. Fifty-three percent of individual contributors surveyed said that they don't feel safe expressing their opinions.[6] If you're leading a team, know that, statistically speaking, half of your members are holding back their true thoughts out of fear. This is a serious issue as it stifles honest communication and hinders team collaboration.

Conflict Resolution

As wisely stated about Margaret Heffernan, "For good ideas and true innovation, you need human interaction, conflict, argument, and debate."[7] There is no true collaboration without conflict. Period.

Conflict is inevitable, but it doesn't have to be destructive. I'm not talking about mean-spirited, nasty confrontations. The problem with conflict isn't that it gets nasty; it's that we are afraid of it going there, so we avoid it at all costs, leaving important issues unaddressed and unresolved.

---

6   Wiley, "Wiley Workplace Intelligence Annual Report: Top 10 Takeaways from 2023," *Everything DiSC* (blog), January 25, 2024, https://www.everythingdisc.com/blogs/wiley-workplace-intelligence-annual-report-top-10-takeaways-from-2023/.

7   Cassity Jakovickas, "How Workcase Conflict Can Help Your Firm," Karbon Magazine, accessed December 9, 2024, https://karbonhq.com/resources/workplace-conflict-can-help-your-firm/.

To help people leverage this powerful dynamic on the team, leaders and teams need to let go of certain beliefs about conflict. Let's do a quick true or false quiz to test your beliefs:

1. The most successful teams have very little conflict.
2. The best teams always achieve consensus when making decisions.
3. No matter their background, people generally prefer to avoid conflict.

How do you think you did?

- The first statement is **false**. Productive teams don't shy away from conflict; they actively engage in debate and share their opinions. These teams become comfortable being uncomfortable because they're focused on the big picture. They know that good ideas come from hashing things out, not from avoiding conflict.
- The second statement is also **false**. Great teams don't need consensus; they need agreement. Why? Because achieving consensus is incredibly difficult and usually means that someone had to give in to avoid tension. Instead, focus on reaching a point where everyone can collaborate even if they don't completely agree. The team debates behind a closed door, but when that door opens, everyone's on the same page. So, agree to disagree, and move forward.
- The third statement is—maybe you guessed it—also **false**. Plenty of people don't shy away from conflict. Some actually get energy from it. They're the ones who love stirring the pot and pushing boundaries. Conflict, in the right doses, can be a source of creativity and motivation.

For me, often the best ideas come from conflict. I tend to be the kind of collaborator who speaks directly and sharpens my thoughts by discussing them. I often find that engaging with a differing opinion sparks new ideas and insights, even if it initially creates some friction. Tension tests my thinking, helps me rationalize, and solidifies my commitment.

So, you probably know what's coming up next: because conflict needs to happen, equip your team with tools and support for managing disagreements constructively. Focus debates on solutions rather than problems, and transform conflicts into opportunities for growth. Conflict is inevitable, but when handled well, it strengthens the team.

Here are some strategies to help you create productive conflict on your team.

Normalize Conflict

Share the importance of conflict in team development and the idea that conflict isn't something to fear—it's something to manage. Reinforce that it's okay for team members to disagree and feel tension. It's necessary for the team's growth.

I often like to share the Team Development Curve with teams to help them understand the normal cycle of growth and why they are experiencing their feelings and frustrations. If I observe tension during discussions, I acknowledge that this is what the team is experiencing and point out that this is exactly what needs to be happening.

One caveat: if people are behaving inappropriately, they need to be called out on those behaviors during or after the meeting. We will explore how to engage in these conversations in the next chapter.

Build Awareness of Reactions

One key to navigating conflict successfully is understanding that not everyone reacts to tension the same way. Our personal styles, shaped by our unique experiences and preferences, play a significant role in how we handle disagreements. The DiSC model offers valuable insight into these styles, shedding light on how different team members may respond during moments of conflict.

Each DiSC style brings its own strengths and challenges to conflict resolution. By becoming aware of these tendencies, the leader and the team members can manage conflict more constructively, leveraging the diversity of styles to find better solutions.

For instance, a D style (Dominance) tends to approach conflict head-on, often viewing disagreements as a way to push for results. While their directness can be an asset in moving the team forward, it can also create tension if not tempered with empathy for others' feelings.

When collaborating with a D style, remind them that while speed and decisiveness are valuable, it's important to slow down and consider others' viewpoints. Encourage them to listen more actively, and frame the discussion around the achievement of goals. Try saying, "I know you want quick action here, but let's ensure everyone's perspectives are heard so we can make the decision efficiently."

On the other hand, an i style (Influence) might prefer to avoid conflict altogether, focusing instead on maintaining harmony and relationships. While this can help keep the peace temporarily, it can also lead to unresolved issues festering below the surface.

Help individuals with this style feel safe expressing disagreements. Encourage them to speak up when they have concerns rather than defaulting to pleasing others. You might say, "Your input is really valuable. What's your honest take on this situation?" Reinforcing that conflict can strengthen relationships, especially when handled constructively.

Similarly, an S style (Steadiness) seeks stability and tends to shy away from confrontation. They may need more encouragement to voice their concerns openly but can be key to ensuring the team considers everyone's perspectives.

With S styles, create a safe space for them to share their concerns without feeling pressured. Directly invite their input and reassure them that it's okay to disagree. You could say, "I can see you're holding back. It's okay to disagree here—what's on your mind?" Make sure to follow up with them one-on-one if needed, as they may feel more comfortable sharing in private.

Finally, the C style (Conscientiousness) tends to be analytical and detail-oriented, preferring to engage in conflict with data and logic. While their thoughtful approach can be valuable, they might struggle with the emotional side of conflict.

Encourage Conscientiousness styles to express their thoughts in a way that balances logic with empathy. Help them understand that it's not just about being right but also about understanding how their approach impacts the team's dynamic. You might say, "Your analysis is spot-on, but let's also consider how we can present this in a way that helps the whole team get on board."

By recognizing these different styles, you can guide your team through conflict more effectively. Adjust your approach depending on who is involved, helping them feel heard, valued, and safe to express their concerns. Encourage the more conflict-averse styles to share, and remind the more confrontational ones to be mindful of others' perspectives. This understanding helps create a more balanced and constructive team dynamic.

Manage Emotions

This point is a bit counterintuitive for most. We are often taught that the best way to deal with conflict is with logic, but I disagree. Conflict, by definition, is a state of disagreement involving strong emotions. Look, if there is a difference in opinions, beliefs, perspectives, or goals but feelings are not involved, that is simply a conversation. Emotions are what create conflict.

So when you are managing conflict on your teams, try to understand what emotions are triggered and address those with logic. I am not saying that you need to turn into a therapist here, but know your people to understand what might trigger unproductive emotions (okay, that sounded a bit like therapy!).

Here's how you might strike that balance:

Example 1: "Your team is constantly late on deliverables."

Emotion trigger: The person being called out might feel attacked or defensive, which could escalate the conflict.

Suggested approach: "It sounds like you're frustrated with the timing of deliverables. Can we focus on what's causing the delays so we can find a solution together?"

This approach addresses the emotional trigger while steering the conversation toward problem-solving rather than blame.

Example 2: "We never listen to anyone's ideas during meetings."

Emotion trigger: The person feels ignored or undervalued, which can lead to frustration or withdrawal from future discussions.

Suggested approach: "I hear that you're feeling some team members are being unheard, and that's important. Can you share more about it so we can better understand?"

This response acknowledges the person's emotions while refocusing the conversation on understanding and collaboration.

Conflict is a natural and inevitable part of human interactions and necessary for growth, innovation, and evolution. If a team does not engage in passionate debates and call one another out, collaboration and consequently optimum performance cannot be achieved.

Define Roles and Responsibilities

One last thing to consider in the Storming phase is how the structure of the team comes together. As members naturally vie for influence and try to understand the value they bring to the group, it's especially important to establish clarity around roles and responsibilities. Without it, the team risks confusion, overlap, or critical gaps in task execution. Clear definitions help ensure that every necessary task is covered and that everyone understands their unique contribution to the team's success.

Remember the story of my son Tim at his first soccer practice? As the kids progressed from the Forming phase, they understood the objective of the game—to score goals. However, if the coach did not discuss roles and responsibilities on the field, they would all try to be the one scoring. No goalie, no defenders—just a chaotic scramble where everyone is trying to take the shot.

In the same way, a team in the Storming phase can face similar challenges if roles aren't clearly defined and understood by all. Everyone might focus on what they see as most important—like getting the goal!

The Storming phase isn't just tough on your team—it's tough on you too. It's frustrating to watch slow progress or recurring conflicts, but remember, discomfort is part of the process. Allow yourself to feel that frustration while keeping your focus on the bigger picture: helping your team build a foundation for lasting success as they move into Norming and, ultimately, Performing.

ROLE AND RESPONSIBILITY DEPENDENCY ACTIVITY

This activity provides a practical way to help your team gain clarity on roles and responsibilities. I have done this often with clients, and the exercise works very well because it allows team members to clearly communicate their priorities, understand who they depend on, and build a sense of accountability.

Here's how to run it:

1. **In-person or virtual setup:** If you're in-person, give each team member a large Post-it note. For virtual teams, tools like a Miro board work great.
2. **Prompts for clarity:** Ask team members to write down key information on their note. For example:

   o *What is your top priority over the next three months?*
   o *What is your one key responsibility?*
   o *What is a success factor you're aiming to achieve?*

3. **Sharing and mapping:** After they've filled out their note, have each team member place it on the board and share it with the group. Once everyone has shared, ask the team, "Who am I dependent upon for success?" and draw lines between people who are interdependent.

4. **Visualizing team dynamics:** By the end of the exercise, you'll have a visual map of dependencies that not only shows how interconnected the team is but also highlights areas where collaboration is critical.

Here is what the board might look like:

ROLE AND RESPONSIBILITY ACTIVITY

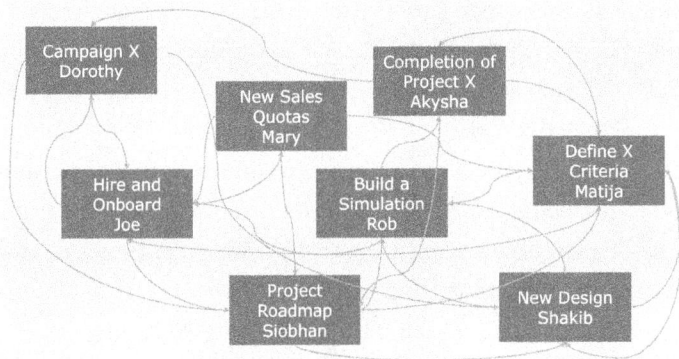

This is a mess, right? It just shows you how interconnected people and teams really are.

I recommend running this activity on a quarterly basis, especially if your company follows an OKR (objectives and key results) cycle. It's a great way to keep roles and priorities fresh in everyone's mind while promoting transparency and accountability. Plus, it helps the team operate more independently, reducing the need for the leader to micromanage or constantly intervene.

NORMING

When the team successfully navigates the challenges of the Storming phase, they naturally move into Norming. This transition is subtle, so be tuned-in to notice the shift. You will see the team begin to find its rhythm. Decision-making gets faster, issues are not rehashed as often, and team members become more task focused and engaged in discussions. Team norms—both those explicitly discussed and implicit—start to solidify, and members develop stronger loyalty to the group. However, not all norms are productive, so it's the leader's responsibility to ensure that the emerging norms contribute positively to the team's success and desired culture.

In this stage, team members feel a greater sense of responsibility and accountability to each other. They're more likely to follow agreed-upon processes, listen to each other's perspectives, and hold themselves and others accountable for meeting the team's objectives. For you as the leader, this is a time to start stepping back, giving the team more autonomy while continuing to provide guidance when needed. You want to shift from directing to coaching, ensuring that the team continues on the right path without needing constant intervention.

Here's what team members need during Norming.

Rules of Engagement

As the team settles into a more cohesive unit, it's critical to solidify rules of engagement. As discussed earlier, in the Forming phase it's important for the leader to set basic guidelines that govern how the team interacts, makes decisions, and resolves conflicts. Now, as the team matures, it's time to refine and define these rules to suit the team's unique dynamics and ensure long-term success. Without clear rules, the team risks slipping into negative behaviors or reverting to old habits.

Keep it simple! Teams only need three to five norms; otherwise, who will remember? Your role is to guide the team in defining and agreeing upon these rules.

What can you do?

Tease Out Existing Norms

By the time your team hits Norming, they've likely developed some norms naturally through Forming and Storming. Plan a one-hour meeting and let the team know that they will be working on the rules of engagement. Yes, you might get some eye rolls (who doesn't love a good meeting about meetings!). Explain how these will help the team to collaborate better, build stronger relationships, and deliver on results without additional stress (intrinsic motivators!).

During the meeting, guide—don't direct—the conversation by asking, you guessed it, open-ended questions. For example:

- What are we currently doing that is helping us succeed?
- Which behaviors or patterns do we think might be holding us back?
- What do we do well when we're at our best as a team?

For example, the team might recognize that they always end meetings with clear action items, which helps with accountability. However, they might also notice that certain team members often dominate discussions, leaving others without a chance to contribute. Capture these on a whiteboard so everyone can see.

Define New Norms for Success

Once you've teased out the existing norms, it's time to define new ones to support continued success. You can do this in the same meeting or host another one—it'll take about another hour. Get the team thinking with questions like:

- What does a highly effective, collaborative team look like for us?
- How do we want to handle disagreements or conflicts going forward?
- What values or behaviors should guide us when we make decisions?
- What's changed in how we work that might require adjusting these rules?

Again capture the output on a whiteboard. When all has been said, ask the team to collapse any duplicates and if you end up with more then five, have the team vote on the ones that are most crucial right now for the team to move forward on the development curve. This is a simple process that does not need a lot of discussion. If the majority feels there needs to be more than five, okay. Let them know these will be revisited regularly to make sure the team lives by them and they evolve as the team's needs change and as new dynamics come into play.

Examples of productive norms that teams may identify include:

- **Assume positive intent:** When giving or receiving feedback, assume that the person speaking is coming from a place of helpfulness rather than criticism. This reduces defensiveness and encourages open dialogue.

- **Be curious, not critical:** When disagreements arise, encourage the team to approach the situation with curiosity rather than immediately jumping to judgment. For example, instead of saying, "That won't work," ask, "Can you help me understand how you see this working?"
- **Collaborate before deciding:** Foster a culture where team members seek input from others before finalizing decisions. This ensures that multiple perspectives are considered and helps to avoid groupthink.

Establishing clear rules of engagement is essential to ensure everyone knows the modus operandi. Remember to keep the process simple and participatory, guiding rather than directing the conversation, and check in periodically to validate if the team is on track or if tweaking is required.

Peer Accountability

In the Norming phase, accountability becomes a shared responsibility. Instead of relying solely on the leader for feedback and correction, team members start holding each other accountable. This peer-to-peer feedback strengthens trust and empowers the team to address issues directly and in real time.

If you are always the intermediary for feedback, you end up spending valuable time on small issues. Encouraging peer-to-peer accountability allows you to focus on higher-level guidance and strategy, rather than micromanaging day-to-day matters.

Peer feedback can feel awkward at first—people often worry about causing tension and damaging relationships—but it's crucial for team members to address issues directly, help one another improve, and create a shared sense of accountability.

What can you do?

- Encourage peer feedback by modeling it yourself. When issues arise, ask team members to discuss them directly with each other first. For example, if someone mentions a missed deadline, ask, "Have you spoken with them about this?"
- Teach feedback frameworks like SBI (Situation-Behavior-Impact) or SAIL (Specific, Ask, Impact, Link; we will explore this concept in the next chapter) to help your team feel comfortable providing feedback in a constructive manner.
- Remind the team that accountability is about supporting each other in achieving shared goals, not about assigning blame.
- Acknowledge and recognize instances where team members effectively hold each other accountable. This could be through verbal recognition in meetings, shout-outs in team communications, or even small rewards.

Peer-to-peer feedback can be the toughest aspect for teams to embrace. But when members of a team find the courage to give honest feedback and push each other toward improvement, you know they're getting close to their optimum performance.

Autonomy

One of your main objectives during Norming is to reduce the team's reliance on you. By now, they should be able to solve problems, resolve conflicts, and make decisions on their own. This can be challenging if you're used to being highly involved, but it's a necessary step for team growth.

What can you do?

- Gradually step back and allow your team to make decisions

and solve problems on their own. Resist the urge to intervene immediately when challenges arise.

- Shift from providing answers to asking guiding questions. For instance, if the team is stuck, you might ask, "What solutions have you already considered?" or "What could be the potential next steps?"
- Trust your team's judgment, and give them the space to learn from both successes and failures.
- Start delegating tasks to the team; for example, let them run meetings by themselves.

The true test is how well the team functions when you're not around. Giving them the space to operate independently is crucial for their growth and long-term success.

Safety Net

As the team enjoys greater autonomy, they may still worry about falling back into Storming, especially if they spent a lot of time in conflict. They need to know that you're keeping an eye on their dynamics and will step in if unproductive behaviors reemerge.

What can you do?

- Regularly check in with the team to ensure that the norms they've developed are still helping them achieve their goals.
- If you notice unhelpful behaviors, address them early. For example, you could say, "I've noticed we're not bringing up controversial issues. How can we create a more open environment for honest feedback?"
- Provide one-on-one feedback when necessary to create self-awareness and develop skills.

Providing a safety net to support the team during challenges or prevent them from regressing into unproductive behaviors is different then hovering or solving every issue for them. Your role is to empower the team to manage conflicts and dynamics on their own while reassuring them that if the situation becomes too complex, you'll step in to guide them. Striking this balance allows the team to grow, develop confidence, and sustain their autonomy without feeling micromanaged.

Opportunities to Collaborate

The Norming phase is where collaboration starts. Team members are now more open to sharing ideas, working together on problem-solving, and taking collective responsibility for outcomes. Leaders can support this by creating opportunities for collaboration and ensuring that everyone's voice is heard. Collaboration doesn't just happen on its own—it needs to be nurtured. By providing the right opportunities, you'll create an environment where your team thrives together.

What can you do?

- Create regular opportunities for team collaboration, whether through brainstorming sessions, cross-functional projects, or peer review meetings.
- Actively invite quieter team members to share their perspectives. For example, you might say, "I'd love to hear your thoughts on this" or "What are we missing that you think we should consider?"
- Encourage a culture of learning from each other, where team members can share their knowledge and skills openly.

Norming is where your team solidifies how they operate, creating rules of engagement, shared accountability, and begin to experience real collaboration. As a leader, you shift from directing to coaching, allowing the team to take on more autonomy while still providing the support they need to avoid backsliding into unproductive behaviors. This is where the team starts functioning as a cohesive unit, setting the foundation for the Performing phase.

PERFORMING

Tada! This is it—the pinnacle of team development where the magic of true collaboration finally happens! The team is thriving, leveraging each other's strengths, communicating openly, and pushing toward shared goals with energy and purpose. This is where the team becomes greater than the sum of its parts.

True collaboration is only possible in this phase because the team has built the trust, psychological safety, and mutual accountability necessary to tackle challenges head-on. Everyone is committed, aligned, and ready to do their best work—together.

As a leader, your role in the Performing stage shifts dramatically. A performing team flourishes when given autonomy and space to operate independently. Trust that your team has reached this stage for a reason—step back and let them do what they've proven they can do.

At this point, it's important to distinguish between a team's optimum performance and meeting set objectives. Many leaders equate success solely with achieving organizational targets, but team performance is not always tied to whether corporate objectives are met. Company goals, set at a higher level, are often influenced by factors outside of the team's control—market conditions, economic trends, or industry benchmarks.

As a result, these objectives can be either too high or too low relative to the team's actual capabilities.

Optimum performance should be seen as an indicator of what's possible for the team, regardless of whether it directly aligns with organizational targets. For instance, your company may set a sales revenue quota of $1.5 million, but your team, operating at peak performance, might be capable of reaching $2.5 million. Conversely, if the economy takes a downturn, the team could perform optimally but only achieve $1 million dollars in revenue. It's critical to recognize that reaching a set goal doesn't necessarily mean the team has reached its potential—nor does missing a target always mean the team isn't performing.

Conflict in Performing Teams

High-performing teams aren't immune to conflict. In fact, because they operate with a strong foundation of psychological safety, they may engage in more frequent, healthy debates. These teams know that challenging each other is part of the process of achieving better outcomes. The difference in the Performing stage is that conflict is handled productively; it's not personal. Team members listen, offer constructive feedback, and resolve disagreements without derailing the team's progress.

Get Out of Their Way

Peter Drucker famously said, "So much of what we call management consists in making it difficult for people to work."[8] This quote reflects the idea that sometimes, instead of facilitat-

---

8   Darin Gerdes, "Peter F. Drucker on Management," The Leadersmith, April 10, 2021, https://www.daringerdes.com/peter-f-drucker-on-management/.

ing progress, leaders can unintentionally create obstacles that hinder a team's ability to perform at their best.

As the team moves into Performing, your role shifts from managing tasks to fostering growth and autonomy. This is the time to delegate bigger tasks and introduce more complex challenges, trusting your team to handle them.

It's essential, however, not to disappear entirely. Instead, focus on offering support when problems arise or when the team explicitly seeks help. Continue to provide resources and encouragement, but avoid micromanaging. Allow the team to learn from both their successes and their mistakes.

Is the Way We Work Working?

Earlier, we discussed the challenge of measuring how the team is performing as a team. The traditional metrics often fail to capture the health of collaboration or the interpersonal dynamics at play. Regular retrospectives and health checks allow the team to not only measure *what* they've achieved but *how* they're working together, uncovering any inefficiencies that could hinder long-term performance.

A typical retrospective helps the team evaluate what's working, what's not, and what needs to change. This process circles back to the team's established rules of engagement. Are these rules still serving the team? Have new "speed bumps" emerged that slow progress or create inefficiencies?

I recommend teams begin conducting retrospectives monthly and eventually move to quarterly, reinforcing what is working well, and making necessary tweaks to support productivity and the desired culture.

CONDUCTING A RETROSPECTIVE

A retrospective is a structured meeting held at the end of a project or sprint (in Agile frameworks) where the team reflects on their work and process to identify what went well, what didn't, and where improvements can be made. The goal is to continuously enhance team performance by learning from past experiences and making adjustments for future work.

Key Components of a Retrospective:

- **Celebrate successes:** Acknowledge what went well, giving the team an opportunity to reflect on strengths and replicate them.
- **Identify areas for improvement:** Pinpoint challenges, bottlenecks, or issues that hindered progress.
- **Actionable takeaways:** Define specific actions the team can take to improve for the next iteration or project.
- **Collaboration focus:** Encourage open communication, foster psychological safety, and promote team learning.

Retrospectives help build a culture of continuous improvement, empowering teams to evolve and adapt by learning from each cycle of work.

While retrospectives focus on broader team reflections, health checks are designed to provide more targeted feedback on specific aspects of team dynamics. Health checks can be conducted more frequently and often focus on particular areas, such as the way the team communicates, efficiency of decision-making, or alignment with goals. They allow for quicker adjustments and more immediate insights, offering the team a way to monitor their collaborative health in real time, without the need for extended sessions. These checks can also be integrated seamlessly during or after meetings, making them adaptable to the team's ongoing workflow.

HEALTH CHECK EXAMPLE

Here's a quick and easy health check process that you can use with your team:

At the end of a meeting, ask each team member to rate their satisfaction with the following questions (using a simple color code: green = good, yellow = needs improvement, red = problematic):

- Did we address all critical issues?
- Were we effective in reaching decisions?
- Did everyone contribute?
- Did we address any tough or difficult topics?
- Did I feel heard?

At the beginning of the next meeting, share the results. If most responses are yellow or red for a particular question, make it a priority to address that area in the upcoming discussion. For example, if team members felt that tough issues weren't addressed, encourage them to bring those issues forward. As a leader, this empowers the team to hold themselves accountable and create solutions in real time.

This process can take as little as two minutes, but the return on investment is significant. It keeps the team engaged, focused, and aware of areas for improvement, without letting small issues snowball into bigger problems.

As teams grow in confidence and capability, leaders can introduce more challenging projects that push the boundaries of what the team can achieve. Keep in mind that external changes—such as new team members or shifts in the business environment—may cause the team to revert to an earlier stage of development. Monitor for these disruptions and guide the team through them to maintain high performance.

So, why is understanding these four phases of team development important in the context of collaboration? Well, there is no possible way a team can work together to solve problems, innovate, and create new value if they are not in the Performing phase. With the team now functioning at its peak, let's explore specific tactics to cultivate true collaboration.

CULTURE OF COLLABORATION

Culture is the invisible fabric that holds a team together—binding their values, behaviors, and shared purpose. It's created through daily actions and decisions, shaping how people interact and how work gets done. Leaders establish culture, whether intentionally or not, by the norms they set, the behaviors they model, and the environments they create.

When we talk about a "culture of collaboration," we're talking about building an environment where people are encouraged and empowered to work together to create value. It goes beyond simply working in the same space or attending the same meetings. True collaboration requires an intentional focus on fostering teamwork that drives innovation and problem-solving. It's a living, breathing dynamic, cultivated by ensuring that people know their purpose, contribute meaningfully, and stay aligned toward a shared goal.

To establish a strong culture of collaboration, four elements need to be in place: people, purpose, participation, and performance. Each element plays a critical role in creating a team culture by design. Let's explore each of these elements in turn.

PEOPLE

Having the right people is the starting point, but it's not enough. Have you ever been part of a "collaborative" meeting where everyone seemed disengaged, with a few dominating voices and others who sat silently nodding?

A few years ago, I worked with a team that looked great on paper. They had the right expertise, experience, and skills. Yet, they struggled to achieve results, and meetings felt more like checklists than actual collaboration. Why? Because even though the team had the right people, they didn't have the right collaborative mindset. Some were hesitant to share ideas, others feared disagreement, and a few simply didn't trust that their contributions would be recognized. It was like having a car with a powerful engine but no fuel—potential, but no movement.

This experience helped me realize that successful collaboration doesn't just happen because you have the right people in the room. It happens when team members embody certain qualities that are a requirement for genuine collaboration. Over the years, I've identified six key attributes that characterize good collaborators.

As I review each one of these, think about your team when they are in a collaboration. How would you rate each person on these attributes?

1. **Participation: They are willing to participate and encourage others to do the same.** This quality is more than just about willingness. In a strong collaborative culture, team mem-

bers also create space for others. They encourage people to contribute, share ideas, and actively engage.

2. **Tension: They embrace conflict in the interest of solving problems.** Solid collaboration requires honest conversions, so team members need to get comfortable with being uncomfortable and allow productive friction to drive better outcomes.

3. **Diversity: They value diverse opinions.** Of course we get the importance of diversity within a team, but winning teams actively seek and value diverse perspectives, backgrounds, and opinions. These teams don't shy away from potential dissent—they intentionally invite input from those who might challenge the idea, knowing that these perspectives sharpen thinking and lead to better outcomes.

4. **Humility: They are willing to let go of their own ideas.** Humility in collaboration means listening to others, acknowledging when one doesn't have all the answers, and prioritizing the team's success over individual recognition. It often requires that team members recognize when another idea is stronger and let go of their own for the benefit of the team.

5. **Recognition: They acknowledge and appreciate the contributions of others.** When team members take a moment to thank someone for their insight, highlighting how their contribution helped the team move forward or simply recognizing the effort behind the scenes, teams build trust, strengthen relationships, and encourage continuous contributions.

6. **Execution: They follow through on their commitments.** Delivering on promises is the backbone of successful collaboration. It's not enough to participate in discussions and agree on a plan; team members must actively take responsi-

bility for their assigned tasks and ensure they are completed to the highest standard. Good collaborators understand that their reliability impacts the team's overall success, and they hold themselves accountable not only for individual work but also for contributing to the collective goals.

These attributes of good collaboration are more than just behaviors; they are culture builders. If you're looking to improve collaboration within your team, you'll need to intentionally cultivate these six attributes. This isn't something that happens naturally—you have to bring these qualities to the forefront. Start by having explicit conversations with your team about what these characteristics look like in practice and why they are essential for successful collaboration.

Ask your team to rate themselves and their collective performance in each area. Where are they strong? Where do they need improvement? This will help identify both individual and team-level areas to focus on. From there, conducting regular health checks (as we discussed earlier) will allow you to keep track of your team's progress, ensuring that collaboration remains strong and effective over time.

Remember, collaboration is an ongoing practice that requires attention and fine-tuning. Having the right people is the beginning, and building productive norms that support a strong collaboration culture will drive the desired results.

PURPOSE

One time, I participated in a project kickoff meeting for a client. One of the participants wanted to enact a rule where everyone kept their cameras on during virtual meetings. Another team member agreed to keep their camera on with the caveat they would be doing other tasks during the meeting; they made it clear that they would not be contributing in any way. So, I asked, "If you don't contribute, why are you in the meeting?"

"Because I was invited and I don't know why," they replied.

Truthfully, my first reaction when the participant answered my question was to blurt out, "Why didn't you ask?" But as I thought about it, I realized, with so much on everyone's plates and meetings scheduled back to back, it's becoming normal to blindly show up to meetings. I get that. But, if we want better, more effective collaboration, we need to change the game.

The responsibility to provide a clearly defined purpose, and connect the team members with it, belongs to the person initiating the collaboration. Everyone must know why they're there and how they contribute to the goal.

To this end, I like using the PPP framework (Purpose, Process, Payoff) that I learned from Wilson Learning as a way to create focus, set expectations, and ensure engagement in meetings. I also use it to kick off any project or collaboration. The framework is simple, short, and one of those magic things my clients comment on. It has gained traction in various fields, especially in IT and business settings, as it helps clarify expectations and keeps meetings efficient.

Purpose: *Why* the team is gathering. It sets the direction and scope of the conversation, ensuring that everyone understands the reason for the meeting and what specific problem, project, or topic needs attention. Having a clear purpose avoids meetings that drift off-topic and keeps participants engaged, knowing exactly what needs to be accomplished.

Process: *How* the meeting will proceed. This part involves laying out the structure or agenda and outlining who will speak, roles in the discussion, what topics will be covered, and how long each section will take. It helps everyone understand the flow, so there is no confusion or mismanagement of time. A well-structured process allows for smoother transitions between topics and ensures all voices are heard within the time allocated.

Payoff: The *outcome* of the meeting—what participants will gain from attending and what decisions or actions will be made as a result. This is the most critical part because it highlights the tangible benefits or results the meeting should produce. Defining the payoff helps to ensure that the meeting has value and provides clarity on the next steps or key takeaways for each participant.

With a clear Purpose, Process, and Payoff, meetings shift from being time-draining tasks to focused, collaborative efforts that link up with something greater.

Many people assume that collaboration always aims for a decision, but that's not necessarily the goal—and this can impact how people show up. If participants believe a decision must be made, they may prematurely push the conversation in that direction, without fully understanding the context or asking the right questions. One of the keys to effective collaboration is being clear about the desired outcome from the start. Are we looking for fresh ideas, gathering input, gaining different perspectives, or seeking alignment on direction? Defining the payoff helps focus the team's energy in the right direction, whether it's brainstorming, refining concepts, or—when appropriate—making a final decision.

When I meet with my clients to discuss leadership development curriculum, my goal is to get input on what they are looking to achieve and their perspective on what the leaders in the organization need. I am not looking for ideas, direction, or decisions—that's my expertise. In this example, my PPP usually looks like this:

Purpose: The purpose of this meeting is for me to gain an understanding of your goals and vision for leadership development and the specific needs and challenges your leaders face.

Process: I prepared some questions to gather your insights, perspective, experiences, and organizational priorities. And at any point I am happy to answer any questions you have for me.

Payoff: By the end of this meeting, I will have the necessary information to draft up a leadership curriculum that meets your organizational objectives. After the meeting, I will share the timelines, and we can book a follow-up meeting to discuss the design.

I state this right at the beginning of the meeting and typically ask a question like, "How does that sound?" or "Would you like to add anything to our discussion today?" to transition to the agenda.

For teams that have more detailed and longer meetings, you might want to have a more specific agenda. Here is an example of one for a quarterly sales strategy development kickoff meeting:

Purpose: The purpose of this meeting is to officially kick off the quarterly sales strategy development process. The goal is to align the team on key market trends, gather initial input on potential focus areas, and establish the next steps for building the sales strategy. This meeting will set the tone for the planning process and clarify expectations around deliverables and timelines.

Process:

1. *Introduction and Overview (Ten minutes):* The team leader will provide a high-level overview of the current market conditions, highlighting new opportunities or challenges to consider for the upcoming quarter.
2. *Initial Input (Fifteen minutes):* Team members will take turns sharing their observations from the previous quarter, including customer feedback, competitor actions, and any emerging trends that may influence the strategy.
3. *Brainstorm Focus Areas (Twenty minutes):* The team will collaborate on identifying potential target segments, sales tactics, and key areas of improvement that should be considered in the strategy development process.
4. *Assign Responsibilities and Next Steps (Ten minutes):* Responsibilities for conducting further research and gathering data will be assigned to team members. Timelines for follow-up meetings and the final strategy development process will be confirmed.

Payoff: By the end of this kickoff meeting, the sales team will have a shared understanding of the process for developing the quarterly sales strategy, including the key focus areas for research and exploration. Everyone will leave with clear roles, next steps, and deadlines, ensuring that the team is aligned and prepared to work collaboratively toward creating an actionable and well-informed sales strategy.

In this example, the leader chose to indicate time allotments for each agenda item. This can be a smart move if you don't know the participants and have not established meeting norms or if you know that conversations get off track.

Keep to time limits. If you don't, in the future, team members will not pay any attention to the timing, resulting in a free-for-all that often leads to a meeting that doesn't achieve its Purpose or Payoff.

While defining the Purpose sets the stage, it's the team's participation that turns intent into action. To drive bold, sustainable change in the world, organizations need people who are willing to raise their voices and take responsibility for shaping the future.

PARTICIPATION

Do you ever feel like your team is stuck in an endless loop of meetings where the same topics are rehashed, the important issues are not discussed, and the real decisions are made offline in one-on-one conversations or in the boardroom after the meeting ends?

A lot of that has to do with how people contribute in meetings. Earlier we touched on the attributes of good collaborators, but there are certain strategies the leader can bake into the team's meeting culture.

I often hear leaders share their frustrations about meetings: "People don't participate" or "They show up unprepared." If you have thought the same, it's worth reflecting on what you can do to encourage more engagement. While clarifying roles and expectations, defining a clear purpose, and creating a collaborative culture (with the six attributes we discussed) go a long way, there are practical and proven steps to encourage participation. Sometimes, it's not only about the participants in the room—setting up the right environment can make all the difference.

Here are some ways to set the stage for better participation.

Keep the Team Size Lean

You might have come across Jeff Bezos's famous two-pizza rule, which suggests that if two pizzas can't feed everyone in your meeting, the group is probably too large. While the analogy has had its share of critique over the years, the core idea is simple: smaller teams lead to more meaningful contributions. With fewer people, everyone gets a chance to speak, and discussions stay more focused and productive.

My ideal size for collaboration is four to eight people. I notice as the team size grows, participation decreases. If the task's complexity and skill diversity requires a larger group, I make sure that through breakouts or small group activities, every voice is represented.

Give Breathing Room Between Meetings

We've all had days where meetings run back to back, leaving no time to reset or even grab a glass of water. It's no surprise that participation dips when people barely have time to catch their breath. A simple solution is to schedule meetings for fifty minutes instead of a full hour, allowing everyone a few minutes to recharge. Make that a norm for your team. With just a ten-minute buffer, people come to meetings more prepared, focused, and ready to contribute.

Use Asynchronous Collaboration Tools

Not every collaboration needs to happen in a meeting. Tools like Slack, Miro, or Google Docs let teams share ideas and collaborate without being in the same room at the same time. These tools can be great for brainstorming, gathering input, or even refining ideas before a meeting, so the time spent together is more focused and productive.

For instance, I often use Miro for brainstorming or prioritizing. This async tool allows team members in different time zones to participate when they feel inspired and when their schedule allows. It gives some the opportunity to think things through without pressure. Remember the needs of the different DiSC styles? Some will do their best when the pressure is off from having to perform in front of team members.

With one of my clients, I did an in-person team-building session that concluded with a list of action items. I wrote these on a Miro board and instructed team members to keep adding their ideas. At the end of the week, I closed the board and asked everyone to prioritize the action items listed. By the time we met in person again, the team already had a prioritized list to discuss and we could focus on creating specific strategies that addressed their issues.

Have a Scribe

Having one person capture key points, decisions, and action items frees everyone else to focus on the discussion without the distraction of taking notes. The scribe doesn't need to document every word but should highlight the most important parts: what was decided, who's responsible, and what the next steps are.

Try rotating the scribe role within the team so that no one person always has the responsibility—it's a shared effort and gives everyone a chance to participate and support the team. Alternatively, there are some AI tools now that do a great job at keeping track of and summarizing key ideas. Doing this takes the pressure off your team members, as no one has to be the scribe.

Either way, having notes creates clarity, makes follow-up

easier, and helps you avoid the dreaded post-meeting confusion, where half the team isn't sure what was agreed upon or what they're supposed to do next.

Don't forget to ask the team members what would help them to contribute more productively. You don't need to be a mind reader. Just ask.

These few practical techniques can boost engagement and ensure that everyone in the room is not only present by actively contributing. Fostering participation becomes less about the burden of facilitation and more about creating an environment where team members feel naturally inclined to contribute. But talking doesn't always equal effective collaboration, which leads us to our next critical component of collaborative culture: performance.

PERFORMANCE

In workshops leaders often ask, "This is all great, Dorothy, but how do we measure the effectiveness of collaboration?" Sometimes, the process is long, and it's hard to gauge its impact until it's too late.

For sure, measuring a team's effectiveness can be tricky, especially when the benefits of the effort are not immediately visible or the outcomes are unknown. And even if the objectives are met, this alone may not truly reflect the success of the collaborative efforts.

We've all heard the saying, "The operation was successful, but the patient died." Achieving a specific goal might not always mean we succeeded. Reaching a project's objectives is important, but the health of the team, the process's efficiency, and the sustainable impact of the outcomes are what really define the success.

At the end of the day, how can we measure success? Here are the criteria I use:

1. **Value creation:** Does the team's output contribute meaningfully to the company's strategic goals? Did the results create value for stakeholders or customers? This is the easiest criterion to measure if clear goals were set at the outset.
2. **Efficiency:** Did the team use resources effectively, and did they complete their work in a way that balanced speed with quality? While time is a component of efficiency, it's not the only factor. Efficiency also encompasses resource management, sustainability, and the long-term impact of solutions. Leaders should assess whether the team is producing quality outcomes without cutting corners or creating unnecessary bottlenecks.
3. **State of relationships:** Are team members working well together? Do they communicate openly and trust one another? Healthy relationships within the team are crucial for sustaining high performance over the long term. Even the best technical results falter if team relationships are strained or dysfunctional.

I encourage my clients to incorporate this criteria when conducting a retrospective at the end of a collaboration. This habit helps the team build strengths, reinforces a healthy collaboration culture, and builds readiness for future initiatives.

LEVERAGING A PEOPLE NEED

At a keynote for an audience of about one hundred people, I asked a simple question: "By show of hands, how many of you met someone today over breakfast who you've never met before?"

To my surprise about 70 percent of the room raised their hands. That might sound normal, except for one important detail—all of these people worked for the same organization in the same area of the business.

I followed up with, "How many of you have been working with someone virtually but just met them in person for the first time today?" Again, about the same number of hands.

Why does this matter? Because, how can we expect to leverage interdependencies when we don't even know the people we're working with? We don't know their strengths, roles, or how our efforts might overlap. Without that knowledge, we not only fail to leverage each other's skills, but we often duplicate work, creating inefficiencies that could have been avoided.

In fact, I see this happen frequently. Teams from different departments, all working in isolation on the same project, are unknowingly pursuing the same goals from different angles. Then, in one of my sessions, they begin discussing priorities, and realize they've been working on the same things, but never communicated about it. It's a waste of time, resources, and potential.

This is why connecting people is one of the new strategic necessities of a modern leader. It's not about being social but helping employees build bridges and a strong network that gives them access to leverage the resources available.

Patrick Lencioni tells us, "It is teamwork that remains the ultimate competitive advantage, both because it is so powerful and so rare."[9] As much as leaders value the power of the collective, they often don't know how to fully harness that potential. And the truth is, competitive advantage isn't just about getting the smartest and the brightest together to create value; it's about how the leader creates the environment where everyone

---

9   Patrick Lencioni, *The Five Dysfunctions of a Team: A Leadership Fable* (Jossey-Bass, 2002), vii.

can bring their best selves forward. When a team transcends individual goals and aligns toward a shared purpose, they can capture their own version of the impossible, achieving more together than they ever could alone.

COLLABORATION SUMMARY

This chapter explores the critical role of collaboration as a cornerstone for team success. It highlights that while collaboration offers a significant competitive advantage, hybrid work environments and weak interpersonal relationships have made it more challenging than ever to cultivate. The chapter discusses the importance of Intentional Leadership in creating an environment where team members can fully contribute and build on each other's strengths. It emphasizes that real collaboration isn't just about working together—it's about aligning diverse perspectives, driving innovation, and building strong, trusting relationships that enable teams to achieve shared goals.

Why Cultivate Collaboration?

Collaboration is essential for maximizing team potential and achieving superior results. It offers several key benefits:

- **Competitive advantage:** Teams that collaborate effectively can outperform competitors by leveraging diverse skill sets and ideas.
- **Drives innovation:** Diverse teams working together generate new ideas and solutions that wouldn't be possible in isolation.
- **Enhances efficiency:** Effective collaboration allows for pooling resources and skills, speeding up processes.

- **Builds stronger relationships:** Collaboration fosters trust and communication, leading to more cohesive teams.
- **Achieves better outcomes:** When people collaborate, they can leverage each other's strengths to solve complex problems and create value.

When to Cultivate Collaboration

Collaboration should be prioritized in key moments to ensure its full potential is realized:

- When projects are cross-functional or require diverse skills
- When a common goal requires multiple perspectives to succeed
- When rapid problem-solving and innovation are necessary
- When there are interdependencies across departments or teams
- When the organization is undergoing major changes
- When new value needs to be created

How to Cultivate Collaboration

Effective collaboration is not automatic—it requires deliberate leadership, especially as teams evolve through the phases of development outlined in the Team Development Model:

- Define clear roles and purpose.
- Build trust and psychological safety.
- Encourage productive conflict.
- Leverage team development tools.
- Conduct regular health checks and retrospectives.
- Set norms for open and constructive communication.
- Create opportunities for cross-functional collaboration.
- Reinforce shared accountability and peer-to-peer feedback.

YOUR CHALLENGE

Your challenge is to use what you've learned in this chapter to cultivate stronger collaboration.

1. Assess where your team is on the talent development curve. Are they newly formed and still coming together? Maybe they've dipped down into the Storming phase? Or perhaps they're in the process of Norming? Or maybe they've reached the point where the team is a smoothly running machine capable of taking on challenges and innovating.
2. Plan out three actions you can take to move the team to a more productive phase. If your team is in Performing, reflect on what is working well and reinforce it with the team.
3. Conduct a Six Attributes of Good Collaborators assessment. How well does your team do in each of the behaviors?
4. Discuss the attributes during your one-on-ones and identify growth opportunities for your employees.
5. Select one strategy from the chapter to use with your team.
6. Conduct a retrospective or health check to gauge how the team is working together.

Collaboration is like a perennial garden. From a distance, you view the garden as a whole and take in the serene beauty. As you move closer, you see the individual shrubs and flowers that make up the garden, each one having different nurturing needs. For the garden to serve its purpose, each plant needs to be given what it needs to thrive.

In many ways, your team is no different. Using the tips in this chapter, you can create a collaborative culture that creates a well-functioning team. But you still need to look closer. In the next chapter, we'll talk about what you can do as a leader to enable the fullest performance in each team member.

Chapter Eight

ENABLE PERFORMANCE

"A leader takes people where they want to go. A great leader takes people where they don't necessarily want to go, but ought to be."

—ROSALYNN CARTER

When you think about great leaders, what truly sets them apart? For most of us, it's about how they inspire and elevate the people around them. They don't simply lead their teams to familiar territory; they push them toward untapped potential, even when the path is uncertain or uncomfortable. Great leaders don't only achieve success—they build it within their people. They know that enabling performance is the highest test of leadership because it requires much more than simply pointing toward a goal. It involves turning vision into action, potential into progress, and talent into high performance.

At its core, enabling performance is a dynamic process. It's not a one-time effort but a continuous cycle that intertwines with every aspect of leadership. It's about guiding your team to results while helping them grow into their best selves. It's an ongoing conversation, a journey that requires you, as a leader, to wear many hats: mentor, coach, challenger, and supporter. Enabling performance is about knowing when to push, when to guide, and when to step back.

This final function weaves together everything we've covered so far. Think of it as a symphony: the vision sets the rhythm, expectations set the tempo, collaboration builds the harmony, and talent development strikes the chords of success. Motivation is the driving force that fuels the melody—it's what keeps the music going, propelling your people forward, even when the notes get complex. At the heart of it all is your ability to bring those pieces together, to coach your people to perform at higher levels than they ever imagined.

As mentioned earlier, to drive this kind of performance, leaders must intentionally integrate three key elements: setting expectations, providing feedback, and fostering development. We've already covered setting expectations and talent development, so this chapter will focus on feedback and how leaders can use coaching to effectively enable performance.

In this chapter, we'll start by exploring the benefits of feedback. When given thoughtfully, it can unlock potential, build confidence, and strengthen the connection between leader and team. Then we'll unpack the purpose of coaching, the power of one-on-ones, and finally the dreaded difficult conversations.

THE GIFT OF FEEDBACK

As discussed, the starting point for optimum performance is clearly defined expectations. Once the goals are established—whether they be behavioral or tactical—the leader must observe progress and then provide feedback.

At its core, feedback is information about a person's performance based on set expectations. And when given with the right intent, it can be one of the most powerful catalysts for personal and professional growth.

Do you remember a time when someone gave you feedback that stung in the moment, but in hindsight you were grateful for? Do you still remember the person? We usually do. An inherent trust develops between us and those who provide honest and sincere feedback. It stems from recognizing that they cared enough to step into a difficult conversation and that their insight, even when hard to hear, is aimed at helping us improve. When giving feedback aimed at genuinely helping their people, leaders build meaningful relationships and foster a culture where learning and growth are encouraged and celebrated.

TYPES OF FEEDBACK

There are two types of feedback: constructive and positive. The purpose of constructive, sometimes thought of as "negative," feedback is to redirect behaviors and actions. On the other hand, positive feedback is used to reinforce behaviors and actions—letting the person know that what they're doing is meeting expectations and encouraging them to keep doing it.

What is the most effective balance of constructive to positive feedback? Studies show that to create and cultivate a positive work environment, one where people are motivated and engaged, leaders must provide more positive feedback than constructive—specifically, at a five to one ratio. Yup, that's right—five positives to one negative!

This doesn't mean that you need to cushion every piece of constructive feedback with five positives. In fact, I don't support sandwiching feedback as it dilutes the message. We need to be direct. The ratio is about the big picture. Think about each employee and consider whether you've given employees a balance of positive and constructive feedback in a way that doesn't shape performance through the negative only. Maybe you're thinking, *What if I don't have anything positive to say?* I see it this way: if a person shows up to work and gets paid and has a satisfactory (or greater) performance rating, that means they're doing something right. So, tell them what they are doing well.

There's a caveat here. Employees on a PIP (performance improvement plan) might require a more constructive than positive feedback approach. But we still need to deliver reinforcing feedback when they show effort or progress. Results might not be where they need to be, but the person's attempts to improve need to be acknowledged.

Both types of feedback have a specific purpose. Be intentional about what you want to accomplish and follow simple guidelines to make the message impactful.

FEEDBACK GROUND RULES

Giving feedback can feel like navigating a minefield—and the message can be easily misunderstood or rejected. But when done right, feedback becomes one of the most powerful tools for growth. Before diving into these conversations, set yourself up for success with some fundamental ground rules to manage conflict and keep the discussion productive and focused on improvement.

Be Specific

Have you ever given someone constructive feedback and felt like you were hitting a brick wall of defensiveness, excuses, and resistance? It's likely that your feedback was grounded in inferences, not observed behaviors, and the person felt judged. By providing specific, fact-based information, you can set the stage for a productive discussion about the issues. Don't speak from assumptions about the person's intention; stick to their actions. When feedback is clear, direct, and based in facts, people know exactly what they need to change and why.

The same is true with positive feedback. The person needs to know exactly what they did so they know what to keep doing. "Good job" is an inference and not considered positive feedback!

The difference between inference and behavior:

- *Inference:* A conclusion or interpretation of someone's behavior or actions.
- *Behavior:* A specific, observable action or event that is concrete, factual, and hard to negotiate or defend.

Here are some examples of inference and behavior for both constructive and positive feedback.

Example 1:

- *Inference:* "You were abrupt and negative."
    - This statement is an inference because it's based on your interpretation of the person's tone or attitude rather than specific, observable behaviors. It doesn't tell the person their specific action when they were perceived as abrupt and negative. In addition, what one person sees as abrupt, someone else might not. When two D styles have a discussion, the S style might feel like the two are in conflict, when in fact the D's are feeling engaged and productive.
- *Behavior:* "During our last team meeting, I noticed you interrupted a couple of people before they finished their thoughts and quickly pointed out why their ideas wouldn't work."

Example 2:

- *Inference:* "The presentation you made last week was really good."
    - Because this is positive feedback, most people receiving it will be happy and grateful, but the reality is that they didn't really learn anything from the feedback. Remember, positive feedback is meant to reinforce behaviors. In this example, the person has no idea what they did well so they can repeat it.
- *Behavior:* "The questions you asked during the presentation sparked really good conversation and addressed some issues we didn't foresee."

Before providing feedback, think through your approach and focus on separating the person from the issue.

Check Your Motivation

Why are you giving this feedback? Will this feedback help the person become better?

As leaders, we sometimes give feedback because we're upset about something that affects us personally. For instance, maybe the person said something that hurt your feelings. Focus on the bigger picture and how feedback will improve the person's performance. If it won't, perhaps that isn't a situation for feedback.

Consider When

An unspoken rule suggests that we must give feedback the moment we observe something. This has shifted somewhat in the hybrid world because sharing feedback requires us to schedule a meeting. It's still best practice to deliver feedback as close to the event as possible.

The only time when this is not the best idea is when you are angry or hurt. Take a beat and process your emotions first. We tend to use more inferences when emotionally charged.

Keep It Single Focused

Feedback is most effective when we focus on one issue at a time instead of layering multiple issues. Addressing too many points at once can overwhelm the person and dilute the impact of each piece of feedback. For example, if a team member is missing deadlines, focus on that specific action rather than bringing up their communication style or work quality in the same conversation.

Likewise, sandwiching constructive feedback between positives can feel confusing and overwhelming. Your people can spot when you do this, and they'll focus on the "but" above all else, instead of walking away from the conversation knowing what is working well and feeling appreciated. And you lost two opportunities for meaningful positive feedback.

Make It Short

Land the plane! When leaders engage in long feedback conversations, circling the issue, it's usually because they're uncomfortable and trying to make it easier on themselves. This doesn't serve the employee. Feedback needs to be concise. It's not about being blunt but getting to the point quickly. Constructive feedback is uncomfortable, no matter how well you do it; there's no need to prolong the discussion.

Plan How

Think through the feedback. Use proven frameworks like SAIL to help you prepare and navigate conversations.

If you don't remember all of these ground rules, just remember the first one: be specific. This guideline will help you create a productive setting, where the person is open to feedback, leading to faster, more effective outcomes. This rule is also the first step in the SAIL feedback framework.

SAIL MODEL

The SAIL model is a focused feedback framework that helps leaders achieve the desired results by providing a clear, structured approach through which the message is heard, understood, and then acted on. It is used to provide positive and constructive feedback.

Why the sail analogy? Just as a captain steers the yacht (yes, in my mind it's a sixty-footer), leaders steer their teams toward growth and success with thoughtful, well-planned feedback. When preparing to sail, you start by determining your destination, then chart the course and gather the provisions to ensure a smooth and safe journey. But as with any voyage, how you reach your destination depends on the conditions—sometimes the waters are calm, and other times you're navigating rough seas. The SAIL model helps you prepare and plot your course so you can steer the conversation based on what the other person says. With the right preparation, you'll be ready no matter what the conditions bring.

As in sailing and life, *80 percent of your success is in preparation and 20 percent in execution.* This is where the concept of go slow to go fast plays a huge role. Take a few minutes to prepare, and you will get to the desired results faster and with greater ease.

Now, I don't recommend you script your conversation; that would be like assuming what the weather conditions will be. Instead, think through each area of the model as it relates to the person and the topic you'll be discussing.

SAIL breaks down into four areas: Specific, Ask, Impact, and Link.

- **Specific:** Focus on behaviors, not inferences. Ask yourself:
  - What is the feedback about?
  - Is the topic specific enough? Tangible enough? Task and not person-specific?
  - Is the feedback a potential inference instead of an observed action?
- **Ask:** Identify what you need to know about the situation. Ask yourself:
  - What do I need to know about this situation?
  - What does the employee's world look like?

- What questions should I ask?
- What might be the reason for the situation?
- **Impact:** Determine the value of the feedback. Ask yourself:
  - Why is this feedback important?
  - Why should the person care about this feedback?
  - What is the benefit of giving this feedback or asking the person to change their behavior?
  - How would a change help the team?
- **Link:** Outline the next steps. Ask yourself:
  - What might the person do post-feedback?
  - What support might the person need?
  - How will you know if they're succeeding?

The Link area of the framework does not require you to prepare. You may think of potential next steps, but the actual actions need to come from the conversation with the employee rather than you, the leader.

When preparing, it is helpful to follow the order of the SAIL framework; however, during the conversation itself you may choose to start with different areas. Let me illustrate with an example.

Let's say the desired outcome is to give positive feedback to a team member, Sarah, for her exceptional performance on a recent advertising campaign for a fashion client. Sarah has been with the company for two years and has consistently delivered excellent results. Her role primarily involves managing pay-per-click (PPC) advertising campaigns, optimizing keywords, and analyzing data to improve ad performance.

For the fashion client's campaign, Sarah was responsible for launching a new line of products, crucial for both her company and the client. The campaign had aggressive targets, including increasing website traffic, conversions, and return on ad spend (ROAS). The team had to work under tight deadlines and intense client scrutiny.

Here's how you might prepare for and then conduct this conversation. Prior to the discussion, jot down key points in each step of the SAIL framework:

- **Specific:**
  - ○ Sarah's role in managing PPC campaigns, specifically her optimization of ad copy and keyword selection.
  - ○ A 20 percent increase in ROAS, surpassing the client's expectations.
  - ○ Boosted click-through rates and conversions.
  - ○ Motivated and focused the team under tight deadlines.
  - ○ Handled client demands and feedback with professionalism and poise.
- **Ask:**
  - ○ What did you learn from this campaign?
  - ○ What did you enjoy the most/least?
- **Impact:**
  - ○ Performance impacted the team and company, opening new opportunities in the fashion industry.
- **Link:**
  - ○ Explore key takeaways that can be used in other projects.

Then, during a one-on-one meeting, engage in the feedback conversation. You could start by expressing appreciation for Sarah's hard work and dedication. You might say something like, "I wanted to talk to you today about your exceptional work on the fashion client's campaign. Your strategy and execution were outstanding." From here, you can launch seamlessly into the SAIL framework:

1. **Specific:** "Your optimization of the ad copy and selection of keywords led to a significant increase in click-through rates and conversions. The campaign's ROAS exceeded the client's expectations by twenty percent." A leader might also include behavioral accomplishments: "Your leadership within the team, helping to keep everyone focused and motivated, was also evident. Your ability to handle the client's demands and feedback was remarkable."

2. **Ask:** "How did you feel about your accomplishments? What did you learn? What did you enjoy the most? What did you enjoy the least?"

3. **Impact:** "This campaign was important for our team and the company. This is the first time we worked in this industry, and your success opens the door to pursue this market segment moving forward."

4. **Link:** "Now that the project is closed, is there anything you learned that you want to use in other projects?"

In this case of positive feedback, Sarah walked away with clarity on what went well and with ideas on how she can challenge herself or learn new skills in the future. And you, as the leader, gain deeper insights into how Sarah felt about the project, what she learned, and her motivators and demotivators. A win-win for both.

Now let's conduct a constructive conversation. Pat is a smart, results-oriented employee whose contributions you value and who models many good behaviors for the rest of the team. You're having this conversation because during the last team meeting, you noticed Pat interrupted another team member, Alex, midthought. Frustrated, Alex reacted by saying, "Pat, please let me finish." Pat responded with, "We've heard all of this before." Alex became disheartened and remained quiet for the rest of the meeting.

Here is your preparation:

1. **Specific:** Pat interrupted Alex, and when Alex asked Pat to let him finish, Pat answered with, "We've heard all of this before."
2. **Ask:** How did you feel when Alex talked about the project? Why? Did you notice the impact your comment had on Alex?
3. **Impact:** All team members need to be heard. Teamwork is important. If people feel they cannot express their true opinions, they will be reluctant to participate and this in turn can impact Pat's and the team's results.
4. **Link:** Perhaps suggest that Pat ask questions instead of making statements or that he discuss frustrations with the team members offline.

Before the conversation, consider the best point of entry, not based on your preference but on your understanding of the person you're giving feedback to. If you think the person will not have a lot of awareness about their own actions and the situation in general, start with Specific. If you think the person has awareness and will be open to the conversation, start with Ask. If you expect the person to resist the feedback and defend their position, start with Impact.

Let's play out each approach. The order of the SAIL steps is identified at the beginning of the example.

Example 1: Specific—Ask—Impact—Link

Leader: "Pat, I wanted to talk about our last team meeting. I noticed you interrupted Alex when he was speaking about his project, and it cut off his idea before he had the chance to finish." *(Specific)*

Pat: "Yeah, Alex keeps bringing up the same issue every meeting."

Leader: "How do you think Alex felt after you interrupted him?" *(Ask)*

Pat: "I could see he was upset, but I don't have time to sit in meetings and talk about the same thing, again!"

Leader: "I can understand that frustration. Perhaps there is a different way to solve the issue, but when you interrupt, it can make others feel like their input isn't valued, which could affect their willingness to contribute to future discussions. We need everyone to feel comfortable sharing their ideas." *(Impact)*

Pat: "I get that, but sometimes these meetings just drag on. People take too long to get to the point, and it feels like we're not making progress."

Leader: "I hear you, Pat. Efficiency is important, but the best results happen when everyone has a chance to participate fully. When we allow everyone to express their thoughts, we might uncover insights we would have missed otherwise, helping you and the team deliver faster results. It's about balancing speed with effectiveness." *(Impact)*

Pat: "Okay, so next time I will stay quiet."

Leader: "Staying quiet isn't the goal either. You have valuable input, and we want to hear it too. Maybe there's a more constructive way to express your thoughts without making others feel shut down. How about that?" *(Ask)*

Pat: "I guess I can talk to Alex offline and try to understand what's going on?"

Leader: "Yes, that would be great. You could also ask a question during the meeting, like, 'Alex, it seems like you are working through some challenges. Is there anything we can do to help and support you?' What do you think? Which approach would you prefer to try?" *(Link)*

Pat: "I like the question in the meeting. I will try it next time."

Leader: "Awesome. After the next meeting, let's connect and see how it felt and what the outcome was." *(Link)*

This structure is best when the person lacks self-awareness or situational awareness or prefers a direct approach.

Here is another version with a different starting point:

Example 2: Ask—Specific—Impact—Link

Leader: "Pat, how do you think the last team meeting went? Did anything stand out to you?" *(Ask)*

Pat: "I was a little frustrated, honestly. Alex kept going over things we've already discussed, and it felt like we weren't getting anywhere."

Leader: "I noticed that, too, specifically when you interrupted Alex while he was sharing his thoughts. Cutting in like that shut down his idea before he had the chance to fully express it." *(Specific)*

Pat: "Well, I don't have time to sit there and listen to the same things over and over. Someone has to move things along, and it's frustrating when no one else does."

Leader: "I get that, but when team members are interrupted, it can discourage them from contributing again. When people feel like their input isn't valued, it affects the overall team dynamic and ultimately impacts your and the team's ability to achieve their goals." *(Impact)*

Pat: "I see your point. But we can't just keep talking about the same thing."

Leader: "Let's try a different approach. Instead of interrupting, what if you asked a question to better understand what they're saying? Something like, 'Alex, it seems like you're working through some challenges. Is there anything we can do to help?' That way, you're engaging without shutting down the conversation. How does that sound to you?" *(Link)*

Starting with Ask is often preferred by leaders, but a word of caution. What if the employee has no awareness of the situation? For example, what if Pat said, "The meeting went great. We kept things on track and moved along swiftly." The leader would need to go into the specific behaviors, which might feel like the question was a gotcha. This sometimes creates a gap between the leader and the employee, impacting trust down the line.

Example 3: Impact—Specific—Ask—Link

Leader: "Pat, as you know, teamwork is very important in our department and we are working to create an environment where people do not hesitate to share their ideas. We want input and honesty so our results can be achieved better and faster." *(Impact)*

Pat: "Yeah, I get that. But sometimes it feels like people drag the conversation on too long when we've already covered the points."

Leader: "Can you give me an example of where you felt the discussion dragged on?" *(Ask)*

Pat: "During the last meeting, it was Alex. He basically was saying what he said in the meeting before and probably the meeting before as well. As far as I am concerned, he is trying to get out of doing the project."

Leader: "Yes, I noticed that during the meeting, you interrupted him when he was speaking about his project, and it cut off his idea before he had the chance to finish." *(Specific)*

Leader: "Why do you think he is trying to get out of doing the project?" *(Ask)*

Pat: "Because the project is not moving forward, and all he is doing is talking about the problems he is facing."

Leader: "Could it be anything else that has him at a standstill?" *(Ask)*

Pat: "Well, I guess it's possible. Maybe he's stuck and doesn't want to admit it, or he's feeling overwhelmed with everything else on his plate. I just don't see him making any real effort to push forward."

Leader: "Pat, on our team, we need to work together. Alex's project, if not completed on time, will have an effect on your deliverables." *(Impact)*

Pat: "I know, that's why I was frustrated. So what's the solution?"

Leader: "Can you suggest anything?" *(Ask)*

Pat: "How about I talk with Alex and find out what he needs to move the project forward? And apologize for how I reacted in the meeting."

Leader: "Sounds like a good plan. Let me know after the conversation how it went. When do you plan to do it?" *(Link)*

Pat: "Tomorrow, when we are both in the office. I will connect with you by the end of the day."

Leader: "Fantastic, Pat. This really demonstrates how dedicated you are to the team's success. Understanding Alex's challenges and supporting him will help you stay on track with your goals. Thank you for taking the initiative." *(Impact)*

This approach is very effective when you anticipate the employee will resist feedback or will not agree with the need for it. Be prepared to go back to the Impact step often, as doing so helps to increase the importance of the conversation and keeps the conversation grounded in shared goals. Feedback is essential in helping team members understand where they stand, what is going well, and what needs to change, but it's only the beginning. Once the feedback is given, the next step is guiding them toward that change. This requires coaching.

THE PURPOSE OF COACHING

While setting expectations and providing feedback offer clarity, coaching is the bridge that turns these elements into lasting improvement and performance. Coaching helps individuals grow, stretch, and reach their full potential.

So, what is coaching exactly? I could write a whole book answering that question. In short, coaching is the process of working with an individual to help them discover their full potential by enhancing their skills, self-awareness, and performance. A great analogy dates back to the time when a "coach" was literally a carriage pulled by horses, designed to transport people from point A to point B in comfort.

Now, "comfort" doesn't mean coaches don't stretch their people. They do, because that's when learning happens, but they also know how far to push. Good coaches find an equilibrium between stretching and learning by knowing their employee's motivators, ability and capability limits, and their aspirations.

Coaching is not an occasional intervention, but a continuous presence throughout the performance enablement cycle. It ensures that the processes of setting expectations, providing feedback, and facilitating development are dynamic and tailored to individual needs. Coaches work closely with employees to navigate their career paths, enhance their strengths, mitigate challenges, and ultimately achieve their full potential within the organization.

COACHING VERSUS FEEDBACK

Coaching and feedback might seem similar, or even redundant, but they serve different purposes, and leaders must know how to utilize each at the appropriate time.

COACHING	FEEDBACK
Future focused	Past focused
Establishes goals	Keeps track of progress
Longer discussion	Shorter discussion
Ask directed	Tell directed

THE DRIVE COACHING MODEL

Throughout this book, I've introduced several models and frameworks for leadership. There's a method to my madness: models help break down complex processes, making them easier to understand, apply, and ultimately, remember. Research shows that using structured approaches helps improve learning and retention, providing leaders with the tools to repeat their successes and drive consistent results—the key components of Intentional Leadership.

The DRIVE coaching model serves as both a practical framework and a powerful tool for leaders to guide their team members to the desired destination, safely and comfortably. Through each step of the DRIVE process, you help your people grow, navigate challenges, and achieve their goals. When used correctly, this model enables team members to steer their own success with clarity and confidence.

Here are the elements of the DRIVE model:

- **Desired Outcome (D):** What do we want to accomplish during the coaching conversation?
- **Reality (R):** What is the current state? What are the specific observables?
- **Inquire (I):** What questions need to be asked? What do we need to explore?
- **Value (V):** What value will the change create for the coachee or the organization?
- **Evaluate Success (E):** How will progress be monitored and measured?

Let's consider each part carefully and use it to prepare for a coaching conversation.

The first step is **Desired Outcome,** which clarifies what you want to accomplish during the conversation—your goal. Ask yourself, *Why do I want to have this conversation? What's driving the need for the conversation?*

Here are some common desired outcomes:

- Increase participation or willingness to engage
- Create awareness around certain behaviors and their impact on others
- Develop someone so they are ready for the next level
- Promote ownership, decision-making, and willingness to take that extra step
- Increase performance so the employee meets job expectations
- Build interpersonal skills so the person becomes an effective collaborator

This is by no means a complete list. As we discussed earlier in the "Feedback" section, it's helpful to keep the conversation single focused. When we have too many goals, we are less likely to move forward on any. Having a clearly defined desired outcome ensures both you and the employee are aligned on the goal before diving into solutions.

The next step is **Reality**, or understanding the current state. What specific observables are informing the desired outcome?

In this step, it's important to stick with factual observations and avoid inference or judgment, similar to providing feedback. For example, if the desired outcome is to promote ownership, the leader can provide specific instances where the employee could have demonstrated initiative but didn't, for example, "I noticed that when we received the client's email yesterday, you waited for me to respond rather than replying. I feel confident in you having the information and the knowledge to handle such situations."

Remember to separate the person from the issue to avoid making inferences that could negatively affect your coaching conversations.

Next is **Inquire**—what questions do you need to ask to gain a deeper understanding and have a meaningful conversation, opening the door to self-awareness and growth?

Before the coaching conversations, brainstorm open-ended questions that explore the coachee's feelings, thoughts, and opinions. Here's a list of my go-to coaching questions for different situations:

Creating self-awareness:

- What's one challenge you've overcome, and how did you do it?
- What one strength do you depend on a lot at work?
- What did it feel like to work on the project?

- What steps would you take to solve this issue if I weren't available?

Exploring growth and aspirations:

- What projects would you like to work on or be more involved in?
- What's something you're itching to try that you haven't had the time or resources to do?
- What is a big, audacious goal that you'd like to achieve this quarter?
- What are you passionate about, personally or professionally?

Checking motivation and satisfaction:

- Is your job what you expected when you accepted it? If not, where has it differed?
- On a scale of one to ten, how happy are you at work?
- What's your least favorite part of your day-to-day at work?
- What's something past managers have done that's inspired and motivated you?

Exploring needs and support:

- What would you like more feedback about?
- Where would you like me to be involved more/less in your day-to-day?
- What's top of mind right now that we haven't talked about yet?
- If you were a hiring manager for our team, what role would be your next hire?

Addressing challenges and concerns:

- What's something you'd like to share but is a little stressful to bring up?
- What are you least clear about, in terms of our company-wide strategy and goals?
- What stresses you?
- What, if anything, feels harder than it should be in your day-to-day work?
- If you were managing the team, what would you do differently?

As Bono famously said in his book, *40 Songs, One Story*, remember the power of curiosity and open-mindedness in conversations.[10] When questions, especially the right questions, are not asked, we may operate under the false assumption that we already know the answers. In coaching, asking the right questions is a way to cultivate self-discovery, foster growth, and strengthen the relationship between yourself and your employees.

After Inquire comes **Value**—what value will the conversation, and any actions agreed to, create for the coachee, the team, or the organization? In other words, who cares about this topic? What is the benefit of having this conversation between you and the employee? If the desired outcome comes to fruition, what difference will it make?

The final step is **Evaluate Success**, which focuses on tracking and measuring progress. In other words, how will you know if the coaching has been successful? When done well, this step increases accountability and motivation because it clarifies what

---

10   Bono, *Surrender: 40 Songs, One Story* (Alfred A. Knopf, 2022), 108.

needs to be done and by whom. In some more complex situations, this step may require a more formal action plan and follow-through, in which case try not to jump in and do it yourself, but rather ensure the employee owns the plan. As the old adage goes, we get what we measure, so ensure that this step aligns with the desired outcome and drives sustainable growth in the right direction.

Earlier, we mentioned Sarah, who was responsible for launching a new line of products—a crucial project for both the client and the agency. She received well-deserved positive feedback for her excellent performance on a high-profile advertising campaign. Her strategic approach exceeded client expectations and increased the return on ad spend by 20 percent.

However, although Sarah is still delivering great work, you've recently noticed a subtle change in her demeanor. She seems less enthusiastic and doesn't contribute in meetings the way she used to. Her energy isn't quite the same. You want to have a coaching conversation to explore what's happening and help Sarah regain her motivation and excitement for her work.

To prepare for the conversation with Sarah, you could use the DRIVE framework and jot down a few notes for each element:

- **Desired Outcome:** The desired outcome is to explore what might be affecting Sarah's motivation, energy, and enthusiasm, and to help her reconnect with her work and aspirations, ensuring she continues to grow. It's also to assess whether this change is due to burnout, external factors, or possibly a lack of challenge in her current role.
- **Reality:** Sarah's work remains excellent, but her behavior in meetings has shifted. She is quieter, less engaged, and less enthusiastic than before.

- **Inquire:** "What aspects of your role have been most energizing or draining lately?" "Do you feel like you're getting enough challenges in your current projects?" "What is your workload like?"
- **Value:** Emphasize the benefits of Sarah's continued growth, both for her career and for the team's success. It's important for Sarah to see the value in staying engaged and motivated—not just for her own personal growth but also for the continued success of the team and the organization.
- **Evaluate Success:** Ask Sarah how she would like to proceed.

This simple and efficient framework ensures that you address all the critical aspects of the coaching process, guiding the coachee from point A to point B with clarity, support, and comfort.

In most cases, you will be the one initiating a coaching conversation with a team member. But what if the employee comes to you? In these coachee-initiated moments, you may have no time to prepare as discussed above, but if you are familiar with the DRIVE model, you can still navigate that unanticipated discussion with greater success by hitting on each step during the conversation.

The **D** or Desired Outcome must be established regardless of who initiates the discussion. You have to know what you want from the conversation. It's easy to veer off into stray territory, but try to keep the discussion focused on a single issue as much as possible.

If you are in this type of impromptu situation and you're not clear on the Desired Outcome, you might ask some of the following questions:

- "What's the most important thing for us to focus on today?"

- "What outcome would be most helpful for you after our discussion?"
- "What challenges or concerns are you facing that we need to address?"

You also need to understand the current state, so the **R** or Reality needs to be explored. Here are some sample questions:

- "How do you see the situation?"
- "What is working well?"
- "What frustrates you?"
- "How might others see the situation?"

The **V** or Value of the conversation can help you understand the importance of the issue, and often it crystallizes for the coachee why they need to address it. Some questions to tease out the value:

- "Why is this important for us to discuss?"
- "What would be the impact of this?"
- "How might this help you?"
- "What will be different if this changes?"

When the coachee initiates the conversation, you need to be very much in the flow of the conversation, and a good set of questions can be very useful. Here is an example where the leader doesn't have time to plan, but the DRIVE model still provides the structure for navigating the conversation.

Let's say John, a project coordinator on your team, approaches you unexpectedly, saying, "I'm feeling overwhelmed with my current workload, and I'm not sure how to prioritize everything. Can we talk?"

Desired Outcome (D):

Leader: "John, I'm glad you brought this up. Let's help you prioritize your tasks and ensure you're feeling less overwhelmed by the end of this conversation. How does that sound?" *(Objective: Verify that this is the coachee's desired outcome.)*

Inquire (I):

Leader: "Have you felt like this before?" *(Objective: Check in to see if the employee has the ability and willingness to handle the workload.)*

Reality (R):

Leader: "Tell me more about your current workload. What tasks are on your plate right now, and what's making it feel unmanageable?" *(Objective: Understand the current load.)*

Inquire (I):

Leader: "What do you think is the main factor causing you to feel overwhelmed? Is it the number of tasks, the deadlines, or something else?" *(Objective: Understand if it is specific tasks that are creating a backlog or if it is the overall load. If related to specific tasks, identify ability and willingness for each.)*

Value (V):

Leader: "Prioritizing effectively will help not only manage your time better but also ensure that you deliver high-quality results on the most important tasks. It will help you feel more in control and allow us to meet the team's goals effectively." *(Objective: Help motivate John to keep working toward a solution.)*

Evaluate (E):

Leader: "How about we review your tasks together and identify which ones are top priority and which ones can be delegated or moved? We can follow up in a week to see how things are going. Does that sound like a good plan?" *(Objective: Support John by helping him to understand priorities and unblock barriers.)*

No matter if the conversation is coach or coachee initiated, the coach is responsible for ensuring each DRIVE step is touched on and explored. Equally important is the coach's approach during the conversation.

COACHING APPROACHES

Before you engage in any coaching conversation, you need to consider two key factors:

- Will the coachee respond better to an asking or telling approach?
- What is the coachee's communication style?

Knowing what approach to take may be a little more challenging if the coachee unexpectedly comes to you, but if you have spent the time to get to know your people, you will have some sense of their skill level, personality style, and communication preferences. All of this information will help you approach the discussion in a way that creates a positive, results-oriented environment and connects with the person in a meaningful way.

Let's start with the first consideration: Should you give direction or ask questions?

Tell or Ask

Ready for this? Micromanagement is good! Yup, you heard that right. "Micromanagement" is often seen as a bad word in leadership. But what if, in certain cases, it's exactly what the employee needs?

The truth is, there are times when we all need a more hands-on, prescriptive approach. Everyone, at some point, benefits from closer guidance, especially when learning new skills or navigating unfamiliar challenges. It's not about hovering over someone's every move but about providing the right level of support and autonomy based on their ability and willingness at any given moment.

I created the Ability and Willingness Matrix to help leaders identify when employees need more directive support and when they might benefit from open-ended questions.

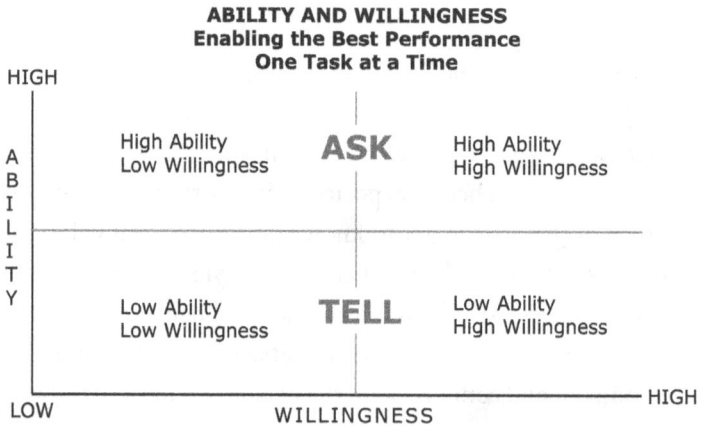

ABILITY AND WILLINGNESS
Enabling the Best Performance
One Task at a Time

HIGH		
High Ability Low Willingness	**ASK**	High Ability High Willingness
Low Ability Low Willingness	**TELL**	Low Ability High Willingness
LOW	WILLINGNESS	HIGH

(Vertical axis: ABILITY)

First, it's important to note that this matrix is task-based, not person-based. It focuses on the specific skills and motivations required for a particular task or project, rather than making broad assumptions about a person's overall capabilities or personality.

The **Ability** axis measures an employee's current skill level or competence in completing a task or meeting a responsibility. On one end, you have employees with low ability, who may lack the experience or skills necessary to complete the work independently. On the other end, there are those with high ability, who are well-equipped and proficient in their roles. When evaluating where an employee fits on this axis, assess their past performance and ask yourself, *Have I seen this person demonstrate this skill consistently?*

Ability isn't about capability or intelligence. It's simply a question of whether or not the person can perform the task right now. For example, I would like to learn pickleball; yup, I am one of the few who hasn't yet. Therefore, my ability to play the game is low. It doesn't mean I won't become great at it, but right now I don't have the skill. And just because I play tennis, doesn't mean I can play pickleball; it might help, but at this point my pickleball ability is low.

One final point here: knowledge doesn't mean skill. I can read a manual about how to drive a car, but until I get behind the wheel and drive successfully, my ability is still considered low.

The second axis, **Willingness,** measures an employee's motivation, desire, and readiness to take on the task. On the low end, you might have someone who is resistant or unmotivated—whether due to lack of interest, burnout, or other factors. On the high end, there are employees who are enthusiastic, committed, and eager to take on challenges. This axis reflects the emotional and psychological drive behind completing tasks.

When the Ability and Willingness axes are crossed, they create four distinct areas, each representing a combination of an employee's current skill level and their motivation to engage with the task. These quadrants guide leaders in how to adapt their coaching approach, specifically, whether they lead the conversation with questions or with statements.

Let's break down each to understand the best way to engage and support your team members.

Low Ability, Low Willingness

These are the tasks in which someone lacks skill and doesn't care about learning it. If you have been trying to schedule a meeting with an employee about a specific issue but they avoid it because they have more important things to do, chances are that issue you want to discuss is Low Ability, Low Willingness for that person. Everyone has areas that fall into this quadrant; there's no judgment here.

For tasks in this quadrant, individuals need clear direction and support, which calls for a *telling* approach. Leaders should provide step-by-step guidance while working to build both skills and motivation.

Low Ability, High Willingness

Employees with tasks in this quadrant are eager to learn and do, but currently lack the necessary skill.

With these individuals, leaders should adopt a *tell-directed* approach, focusing on developing individuals' capabilities while maintaining their enthusiasm.

This area is often a pitfall for leaders as they mistake willingness for ability. The danger with this assumption is that leaders may assign tasks that the employee isn't equipped to handle yet, leading to frustration, mistakes, or missed expectations. While enthusiasm is valuable, it doesn't guarantee the task will be done correctly or efficiently without the skill.

High Ability, Low Willingness

These are the tasks people know how to do; they just don't want to do them. If direct reports regularly whine about or procrastinate in completing certain tasks, that's often a sign that they feel the task is beneath them or the task has become too routine—a classic High Ability, Low Willingness situation.

Here, leaders need to adopt an *asking* approach, digging into why motivation is low and exploring what can re-engage the employee, whether through new challenges or realigned goals. Sometimes just letting them vent about how shitty the task is can go a long way!

High Ability, High Willingness

When employees engage in tasks in this quadrant, you don't see them because they are doing their work and meeting expectations.

In this case, leaders need to take a hands-off approach, *asking* open-ended questions and letting the employee drive the conversation.

When I turned forty, I decided I wanted to do something meaningful to remember that time of my life. So, I decided to run a marathon. The small problem was that I wasn't a runner. My running experience consisted of occasional jogs before holidays, just to fit into a pair of shorts. So, I joined a running clinic.

At first, I was highly motivated but had no ability. I didn't know the first thing about running long distances. My coach took a very *tell-directed* approach, explaining exactly where I needed to start. He told me I needed proper running shoes that would support my gait, instructed me on the basics of breathing, and explained how we'd begin with short runs and walking breaks to build endurance. It was all very prescriptive—one might say he was micromanaging me—but it was exactly the guidance I needed.

But after my first few runs, my excitement started to fade—I went from Low Ability, High Willingness to Low Ability, Low Willingness. I wasn't feeling the rush I expected; running felt hard, and I doubted whether I could actually do this. My coach stepped in and reassured me that this dip in motivation was completely normal. He explained that most people hit this wall early on as they get to understand the full scope of the task. He gave me some practical tips to push through. His *tell-directed* approach helped me build the skills I lacked, and knowing that other runners felt that way normalized my anxiousness.

As I got closer to the marathon, around the twenty-two-mile mark in training, I found myself in a new quadrant: High Ability, Low Willingness. I had the endurance by then, but I was tired and bored. Running was taking so much time from my life, and I started feeling the pressure. At that point, my coach's approach switched to *ask-directed*. Instead of telling me what to do, he asked questions like, "What do you think would help you manage your time better?" He offered ideas but didn't prescribe them. He encouraged me to explore what would work for me, and I started trying different strategies to stay motivated.

Finally, when I completed my training and got closer to race day, I moved into the High Ability, High Willingness quadrant. I was capable, and my motivation was back. At this point, my coach didn't need to tell me what to do—he simply asked, "How was your run?" and celebrated successes with me.

By using the Ability and Willingness Matrix, leaders can better understand what employees need at each stage and with each task. People shift between quadrants depending on the task, the skill level, and motivation. When leaders master their situational awareness around this matrix, they build accountability and support their people from where they are.

When preparing for a coaching conversation, it is helpful to review the desired outcome in the context of the four quadrants. In Sarah's case, the desired outcome is to understand and address the change in her demeanor. Given that she was motivated and engaged before, her ability is high. How about willingness? There has been a change, and if her ability hasn't changed, the problem must be willingness. Based on that High Ability, Low Willingness diagnosis, the most appropriate approach would be *ask-directed*.

MISREADING ABILITY AND WILLINGNESS? NO PROBLEM—SHIFT YOUR APPROACH

Don't worry if you initially misread your employee's ability or willingness during a coaching conversation. It happens! The key is to recognize the signs and make a quick adjustment.

You'll know you've misread the situation if, for example, you ask an open-ended question like, "How would you approach this task?" and the employee struggles to answer or gives a response that you know, from your experience, is off the mark. This is a clear signal that they may lack the ability to proceed on their own.

When this happens, shift your approach. Instead of continuing to ask questions, move into a more directive style. For example, you could say something like, "In the past, we took these steps to tackle a similar problem…" and walk them through a step-by-step process. This provides them with the clarity they need, and builds capability for future situations.

By being flexible and adjusting based on what you observe, you're helping your employees grow and making them feel supported and equipped to succeed.

Communication Styles

To further tailor your coaching approach, consider the coachee's DiSC style. That will help you speak their language, which builds trust, creates openness, and ensures that the conversation is more productive.

There are two places in the DRIVE process where it can be particularly impactful to align with personality traits and communication preferences: at the beginning of the conversation—to create a positive, trusting, open climate—and when outlining the Value.

Here's how you can adjust your conversation starters for each style:

- **Dominance (D)** styles may prefer a direct, results-oriented conversation. They value efficiency, quick decisions, and a focus on outcomes.
    - *How to start:* Get to the point quickly. Avoid too many pleasantries or cushioning, and focus on clear, actionable outcomes.

- *Example:* "Let's dive into the key issue. Here's what I've observed, and I'd like to discuss how we can quickly resolve it and move forward."

- **Influence (i)** styles thrive in a positive, engaging atmosphere. They appreciate connection and enjoy being involved in discussions.
  - *How to start:* Begin with an upbeat tone and establish a personal connection. Encourage open dialogue and create an energizing atmosphere.
  - *Example:* "I'm excited to hear your thoughts on this! Let's brainstorm some ideas about how you can use your strengths to take this project to the next level."

- **Steadiness (S)** styles value stability and support. They work best when they have time to process their thoughts.
  - *How to start:* Start by relating, expressing support, and creating a calm, steady environment. Focus on listening and the relationship.
  - *Example:* "Hi! Thank you for meeting with me. How was your weekend? I appreciate the effort you've been putting in and know the team appreciates it as well. Let's take some time to talk about how we can continue building on that progress."

- **Conscientiousness (C)** styles value detail and precision. They may respond best to a structured conversation that includes data, specific examples, and logical steps, helping them feel clear and confident in their next actions.
  - *How to start:* Begin with a clear agenda and provide specific data or examples. Keep the conversation logical and focused on facts.
  - *Example:* "I've reviewed the data and noticed a few trends. I'd like to walk through these with you and discuss the steps we can take to address them."

And here's how you can use the DiSC styles to tailor your discussion of Value:

- **Dominance (D)** styles value action, results, and efficiency. They need to understand the value in terms of how it will accelerate progress or improve performance.
  - *How to communicate Value:* Highlight the benefits in terms of results and speed. Make it clear how the action will lead to quicker or better outcomes.
  - *Example:* "By making this shift, you'll see faster results and get ahead of the competition. It's a move that will push you closer to your goal."
- **Influence (i)** styles appreciate collaboration, recognition, and creativity. They want to know how the value will enhance the output and bring recognition.
  - *How to communicate Value:* Emphasize how their strengths will be recognized and how the action can positively impact their network and influence.
  - *Example:* "This will not only showcase your leadership but will also inspire the team. I can see everyone rallying around your ideas and energy."
- **Steadiness (S)** styles value support, stability, and harmony. They need to see the value in how it will create a steady and supportive environment.
  - *How to communicate Value:* Show how the change will create consistency and help maintain a supportive team environment.
  - *Example:* "This approach will provide the team with the stability they need, and it will ensure that we're all aligned and moving forward together."

- **Conscientiousness (C)** styles value accuracy, logic, and structure. They need to understand the value in terms of precision and the clarity it will bring to the process.
  - *How to communicate Value:* Focus on how the action will ensure better accuracy, efficiency, or quality in their work.
  - *Example:* "This strategy will help ensure that every detail is accurate and on point, which will save time and prevent any issues later on."

Like the SAIL model, DRIVE doesn't need to follow a rigid step-by-step progression. You can begin where you think is the most appropriate point of entry. For example, if the coachee understands there is an issue, it might make sense to start with Inquire by asking a question like, "What is your perspective on this situation?" If the coachee prefers a direct approach and doesn't know the reason for the conversation, starting with Desired Outcome would probably work the best.

You might also need to move fluidly between steps as the conversation unfolds. For instance, if tensions arise or you are met with resistance, it's always a good idea to circle back to the Value step to reiterate why this conversation is important and how it benefits the coachee. This helps reestablish the purpose and maintains engagement. Similarly, when you enter the Evaluate step, discussing next steps might uncover an unexpected issue or roadblock. In that case, it could be necessary to revisit Inquire to ask deeper questions and better understand the new information.

By remaining flexible and adapting your approach as needed, you can ensure the coaching conversation stays productive and tailored to the coachee's unique needs.

Now, let's play this out using Sarah as an example. Sarah is an Influence (i) style—enthusiastic, motivated by connection, and thriving in positive environments. Because she was motivated before, you know her ability has not changed. So, while she has the ability, her willingness has been low lately. This dynamic suggests that starting the conversation with a supportive tone might resonate best, and the overall approach needs to lean more toward asking rather than telling.

Here's how the whole conversation might go:

Leader: "Sarah, first of all, I want to reiterate how fantastic your work on the recent advertising campaign was. The results speak for themselves, and the client was thrilled. You really delivered beyond expectations, and I've already shared that feedback with you. I want to check in with you and see how you're doing." *(Desired Outcome)*

Sarah: "Thank you. I am doing okay."

Leader: "You've consistently been one of the most engaged and vocal contributors in our discussions, especially when it comes to brainstorming ideas or leading team initiatives. In our last team meeting, I noticed you stepping back, which differs from how you usually show up." *(Reality)*

"Is there's something specific behind that shift?" *(Inquire)*

Sarah: "Honestly, I've been feeling a bit worn out after the big push for the campaign. I haven't had much time to refocus, and maybe that's why I've been quieter. I still enjoy what I'm doing, but the last few weeks have been intense."

Leader: "I completely understand that. After such an intense campaign, it's natural to feel this way. What do you think you need to find your groove?" *(Inquire)*

Sarah: "I just think I need time to get back into my regular job routine."

Leader: "I think you have so much potential, and I want to make sure you're feeling challenged and supported moving forward. Your contributions have made a real difference to the team, and staying engaged is going to help you continue to grow, both for your own career and for the success of the team as a whole." *(Value)*

Leader: "What tasks in your regular job do you find draining?" *(Inquire)*

Sarah: "I like my work; what I really enjoyed was the pace and the high profile of the launch. Even though I was tired, I felt a greater sense of purpose."

Leader: "I hear you. How can you incorporate excitement and a sense of greater purpose into your current role?" *(Inquire)*

Sarah: "Good question; I will need to think about that."

Leader: "Okay, why don't you do that? And also consider if there is anything we can adjust to keep you feeling challenged and motivated." *(Evaluate)*

Leader: "When do you want to check in again and continue this conversation?" *(Evaluate)*

Sarah: "We can do it in our next one-on-one. And thank you for bringing this up. I'm excited to find something that brings that energy back."

By starting with acknowledgment, asking the right questions, and offering space for reflection, the leader created an open environment where Sarah could tap into her motivation and take ownership of her next steps.

One of the most effective places to coach your team members using the DRIVE framework is during regular one-on-one meetings.

ONE-ON-ONE MEETINGS

In our hybrid world, gone are the organic water cooler conversations that brought people together. Today, one-on-ones are the best way for leaders to connect with their people. These structured conversations are an opportunity for leaders to understand their employees on a deeper level and provide the guidance, support, and feedback needed to foster growth. They are also the perfect environment for helping an employee overcome challenges, explore new opportunities, or simply check in on progress. One-on-ones ensure each person receives the individualized support they need to stay aligned with their goals and continue growing.

As mentioned, to enable performance and bring out the full potential in people, leaders need to define the vision, set expectations, ignite motivation, develop talent, build collaboration, provide feedback, and coach. All of these leadership functions can be woven into one-on-one meetings, making them the most powerful tool in a leader's tool kit. Unfortunately, they are so often underused or ineffective. I hear from employees all that time that one-on-one meetings are a waste of time.

Why is that? Often, these meetings fall into a routine of task updates or logistical discussions, when they could be used for so much more. We need to transform these meetings and use them as space to unlock performance, align goals, and build stronger relationships. It's time to reframe one-on-ones—not as a checkbox on a to-do list, but as a powerful driver of growth and engagement.

As with any new practice you introduce to your employees, take time to reflect on whether different expectations need to be set. Launching into new territory can be confusing, especially with all the rapid changes in the workplace. If you plan to approach your one-on-ones differently—whether it's a new structure, frequency, or focus—make sure to clearly communicate this to your team. Setting clear expectations up front will help avoid confusion and ensure your employees feel aligned and comfortable with the changes.

One-on-one meetings exist to help leaders and their direct reports connect, collaborate, and achieve balance. In the following pages, we'll discuss five ways to make one-on-ones more effective.

KEEP THE MEETINGS REGULAR

To make the most of one-on-ones, many of my clients connect with their people for at least thirty minutes every two weeks. Life happens, and sometimes meetings need to be moved or rescheduled, and that's okay—if it's rare. But make it clear to your team that one-on-ones are a priority. Consistency demonstrates to your people that they matter and are valued.

This might be common sense, but it's not always common practice. During a recent training session, one participant shared that at that moment, he had a scheduled one-on-one with his manager that he obviously wasn't attending. When he realized he would be in training during that time, he didn't bother canceling the one-on-one with his boss. Why? Because he and his manager never actually met, despite the meetings being on the calendar month after month. The manager didn't even acknowledge that the meeting was booked. Can you imagine how the employee felt?

Your people need to be and feel like they're a priority in your schedule—and, more importantly, that they matter to you.

MAKE IT THEIR MEETING

The most effective one-on-one meetings are employee-owned. Whether it's seeking guidance, talking through challenges, or sharing updates on projects, this is the employee's dedicated time to bring forward whatever is most important to them. This means that the employee prepares, keeps notes, and initiates conversations.

As a leader, it's easy to dominate these meetings, talking about your priorities or diving into performance metrics. However, the real power of these meetings lies in giving your employees the space to voice their thoughts, concerns, and ideas.

Putting the onus on your employee to guide the conversation signals that you're invested in their success. It allows you to get a true sense of where they are, both personally and professionally, and provides a platform for meaningful dialogue that aligns with their growth and your leadership goals.

But what if they don't prepare or say they don't need a meeting? One-on-ones, as well as the preparation for them, are not negotiable. If employees are avoiding these meetings, it might indicate that they don't see value in them, or maybe the constant follow-up or constructive feedback makes them feel overwhelmed. Whatever the case, the key to building trust and creating value is to lean in and conduct the meetings in a different way.

Here is an idea that has been very helpful for many of my clients: Share a checklist with your direct reports, and ask them to rate each item on a scale of 1 to 5, with 5 being the highest interest and 1 being the lowest. Then ask them to mark three topics that would be of most interest for them to discuss with you. Encourage your employee to add any topics not listed using the blank spaces provided.

During the next one-on-one, ask them which items rated the highest. Start with the most important item. Some topics, like "Things I should know but I'm not aware of," may be addressed in one meeting, while others, such as "The progress I'm making in my career," might need to be revisited over several sessions.

Here is an example of a topics checklist.

ONE-ON-ONE TOPICS CHECKLIST

Please mark the three topics that interest you most on the following checklist. If something important is not listed, add it to the list and mark that as your choice.

	Low			High	
1. The progress I am making in my career.	1	2	3	4	5
2. The success I am feeling in my current position.	1	2	3	4	5
3. How could I contribute more to the organization in my current role?	1	2	3	4	5
4. How could I learn more while in my current role?	1	2	3	4	5
5. How could I expand my role and responsibility?	1	2	3	4	5
6. How to improve the way I work with other departments in this organization.	1	2	3	4	5
7. How my group could be more efficient and productive.	1	2	3	4	5
8. How to gain more technical competence in this industry.	1	2	3	4	5
9. Ways to improve the manner in which I get things accomplished.	1	2	3	4	5
10. How could I become more innovative in my role?	1	2	3	4	5
11. How to achieve better work/life balance.	1	2	3	4	5
12. How to best prepare for career opportunities in the firm.	1	2	3	4	5
13. How to handle a specific challenge I am facing in my work.	1	2	3	4	5
14. How to overcome any major weaknesses that those above me in the organization perceive me to have.	1	2	3	4	5
15. How to identify and magnify those important strengths that I possess.	1	2	3	4	5
16. Things I should know, but I'm not aware of.	1	2	3	4	5
17. Other:	1	2	3	4	5
18. Other:	1	2	3	4	5

If you are thinking, *What about my stuff?* then split the discussion time up into chunks. Different leaders choose different styles of meetings. For example, the 10/10/10 format splits a thirty-minute meeting into ten minutes for the leader to talk, ten minutes for the employee to talk, and the last ten minutes for questions or a wrap-up discussion. That way you still have time to share what's on your mind while giving priority to the employee's concerns.

USE AN AGENDA

Ask your people to come prepared with an agenda or key points they want to cover. This not only ensures that the meeting is productive, but also fosters a sense of ownership and accountability in their role. You can have your agenda points, but they need to take a back seat.

Encourage them to bring up topics such as:

- What's going well in their work and where they see opportunities for improvement.
- Areas where they feel stuck or need support.
- Career aspirations or development goals they want to explore.
- Feedback on how you can support them better as their leader.

For each agenda item, ask the employee to identify what outcome they are looking for; that is, do they want a decision, direction, or information?

For example:

AGENDA ITEM	OUTCOME
Areas I feel stuck	Direction
Feedback on project	Information
Budget allocation	Decision

This methodology helps you to understand what the employee is looking for and allows for you to focus during the conversation in the right direction. For example, if they are looking for information, you will listen to what the employee is sharing through the lens that will enable you to provide the most relevant information.

FOCUS ON THE FUTURE

While it's important to address current issues or challenges, the ultimate purpose of these conversations is to prepare your people for what's next. What are their aspirations? What upcoming projects excite them? What skills do they want to develop?

By focusing on the future, you encourage employees to think about their growth and development, ensuring they continue moving forward in their careers. It also allows you to align their ambitions with the goals of the organization. Use these meetings to discuss not only how they can contribute in the present but how they can evolve in the months and years to come.

Some key questions to explore might be:

- What would you like to accomplish over the next quarter?
- Are there any areas you'd like to develop further?
- What future projects or roles excite you the most?

This forward-thinking approach helps foster motivation and keeps the conversation centered on continuous growth, development, and long-term success.

BE PRESENT IN THE MEETING

This means giving your undivided attention—no distractions, no checking your texts or emails, and no cutting the meeting short. It's about making sure your employee knows they are a priority and what they say matters.

Active listening plays a key role in being present. Engage with what your employee is saying by asking thoughtful questions, summarizing their points, and reflecting on what they've shared. When you demonstrate that you're fully tuned in, you build trust and encourage deeper, more open dialogue.

Additionally, being present also means being mindful of body language and eye contact. Even in virtual meetings, ensure your camera is on and that you're focused on the conversation. Your attention sets the tone, showing that this is a safe, important space for meaningful discussion.

When done right, one-on-one meetings serve as a foundation for building trust, strengthening relationships, and aligning on goals. They create the space to give and receive feedback, foster growth, and enable the team to bring their best selves to work. But not every conversation will be easy. There will be times when you need to address challenges, provide constructive feedback, or navigate sensitive topics.

While one-on-ones are a great place for general development and performance discussions, some conversations—particularly difficult ones—require even more care and skill. Let's dive into how to navigate those challenging conversations, with tools and approaches that can help you turn potential conflict into productive dialogue.

DIFFICULT CONVERSATIONS

Even with careful preparation and the right frameworks in place, difficult conversations can sometimes take an unexpected turn. Emotions flare, defensiveness builds, or the employee may push back in ways you didn't anticipate. As a leader, the key to managing these challenges is knowing how to redirect the moment without escalating the tension.

It's like the martial art of Jiu Jitsu. In Jiu Jitsu, the practitioner uses their opponent's energy and momentum to their advantage. It's not about using brute force or overpowering the other person but about redirecting energy, creating balance, and finding an opening for a productive outcome. Similarly, in a difficult conversation, your role as a leader is not to overpower or out-argue the other person but to guide the conversation toward a solution while managing emotions and tension.

Here's how you can apply the principles of Jiu Jitsu in difficult conversations:

Lean in: Rather than avoiding or minimizing the issue, lean into the conversation. Acknowledge the challenge and ask for the employee's perspective. This diffuses tension and makes the other person feel heard.

Example: Suppose you're speaking with an employee who has been resisting new initiatives. They express frustration and challenge the changes, saying, "This new process is just making things more complicated for everyone." Instead of countering with a defensive response, lean in with, "I hear you. Can you share more about what specifically feels complicated?"

State shared interest: Establish common ground. Remind the employee of the shared goals and outcomes that benefit both of you and the team. This keeps the conversation focused on the greater good rather than personal grievances.

> *Example:* After hearing their frustrations, you might respond with, "I understand this feels overwhelming. I think we both want to make sure the team is set up for success and that the changes are as smooth as possible. How do you think we can make this process easier for everyone?"

Stay calm: Throughout the conversation, focus on maintaining your composure, even if emotions run high. Pause if needed, take a breath, and remember the desired outcome. If the conversation becomes too heated, consider taking a short break to cool off before continuing.

> *Example:* If the employee continues to push back or even gets defensive, it's essential to stay composed. "I can see this is really frustrating for you, and I want us to work through this together. Let's take a moment, and maybe we can find some solutions."

By applying the Jiu Jitsu principles—leaning in, finding shared interests, and staying calm—you can manage even the most challenging conversations without turning them into confrontations.

ENABLE PERFORMANCE SUMMARY

In this chapter, all the leadership Functions we've discussed come together into a cohesive framework that exposes the full potential of people, teams, and ultimately organizations. Enabling performance is often the way a leader's success is measured. It's the core of leadership.

The tools that help leaders successfully navigate this Function include:

1. Providing regular feedback against set expectations using the SAIL model, and keeping a healthy ratio between positive and constructive feedback
2. Engaging in regular coaching conversations using the DRIVE model, ensuring that the desired outcome is clear and progress is measured effectively
3. Knowing when to ask and when to tell, embracing micromanagement when the situation calls for it
4. Tailoring the approach using the coachee's communication preference to create an open, positive climate during the conversation
5. Leveraging one-on-one meetings as an opportunity to add value and build a stronger relationship
6. Building courage to engage in difficult conversations that unblock barriers to success

Why Enable Performance?

Enabling performance is the hallmark of great leadership because it transforms potential into results. Why enable performance? Because it:

- Helps your people grow
- Creates self-awareness

- Motivates your team members
- Improves performance

When to Enable Performance

As leaders, we enable performance by utilizing a holistic approach through which we create an environment where people can discover their full potential and be at their best. This involves setting clear expectations, monitoring how the employee is performing based on those expectations, providing feedback, and creating a supporting and challenging environment. The desired performance is our goal, but balancing results with employee needs is the best way to build a team that not only responds to challenges, but surpasses them.

How to Enable Performance

Here are some of the best methods for getting the most out of your people:

- Monitor employee performance against set expectations.
- Provide positive and constructive feedback on a regular basis using the SAIL model.
- Balance positive and constructive feedback (5:1).
- Coach and mentor with an emphasis on developing using the DRIVE model.
- Spend regular one-on-one time with your direct reports.
- Learn to manage difficult conversations.
- Build self-awareness in your employees.

YOUR CHALLENGE

Here is your last challenge, and this one is a three-parter:

PART 1: TRANSFORM YOUR ONE-ON-ONE

1. *Pick a team member:* Identify someone on your team whose one-on-one meetings haven't been as engaging or effective as they could be. Maybe it's become a task-oriented update, or maybe the employee hasn't been bringing topics forward.
2. *Reflect on past meetings:* Think back on what typically happens during these meetings. What's missing? Is there a lack of meaningful conversation, goals, or future-oriented discussions? Do you dominate the conversation, or does the employee?
3. *Revamp your approach:* Use the checklist method we discussed earlier in the chapter, or simply invite the employee to own the agenda for the meeting. Plan to focus on the future and avoid falling into routine updates.
4. *Schedule the next meeting:* Keep the commitment and show the employee that this time is valuable.
5. *Conduct the meeting:* Be present, listen actively, and use the employee's input to guide the conversation.

PART 2: PROVIDE CONSTRUCTIVE FEEDBACK

1. *Identify a situation:* Think about someone on your team who could benefit from receiving honest, constructive feedback— someone you've hesitated to give feedback to before.
2. *Prepare:* Using the SAIL model, prepare for the feedback conversation. Be specific, ask for their perspective, explain the impact, and link the conversation to future improvements.

3. *Conduct the conversation:* Follow through with the meeting, ensuring the feedback is clear, actionable, and focused on growth. Don't forget to anticipate any potential challenges, and be ready to use the Jiu Jitsu approach if needed.

4. *Review and reflect:* After the conversation, reflect on how it went. What worked well? What would you do differently next time? This reflection is key to improving future feedback conversations.

PART 3: USE COACHING TO DEVELOP

1. *Pick a team member:* Identify someone on your team who could benefit from a coaching conversation. Maybe they're ready for a new challenge or need help solving a problem they're stuck on.

2. *Prepare using DRIVE:* Plan for the conversation using the DRIVE model. Identify the Desired Outcome, assess the Reality, and prepare open-ended questions to drive the conversation. Make sure you understand the value of the conversation for both the coachee and the organization.

3. *Conduct the coaching conversation:* Engage in the coaching session, using open-ended questions to help the employee reflect, explore options, and take ownership of their development.

4. *Ask for feedback:* At the end of the conversation, ask the employee how the conversation went. Did they find it useful? What could be improved in future coaching sessions?

These steps will help you elevate your leadership approach by using one-on-ones, feedback, and coaching to enable higher performance in your team. Each part of this challenge offers an opportunity to refine your leadership style and strengthen your relationship with your team members.

CONCLUSION

As we come to the end of this book, remember that leadership isn't a destination but a continuous journey requiring a commitment to continual growth, learning, and self-discovery. The Six Functions you've explored—Define the Vision, Set Expectations, Ignite Motivation, Develop Talent, Cultivate Collaboration, and Enable Performance—are your foundational tools for effective leadership. These are not one-time actions but ongoing practices that, when used consistently, can transform your approach and your team's success.

You don't need to become anyone to be a good leader. Leadership is about what you do, not who you are. You can learn the skills to be an excellent leader, effecting change on your team and throughout your organization. Just like every superhero who discovers their abilities, learns to harness them, and ultimately uses them to transform the world around them, your journey as a leader is about discovering and unleashing your potential to create meaningful impact.

Your superpower as a leader lies not only in the mastery of these Functions but in your ability to tailor them to the unique needs of your team. You have the ability to see beyond the present and envision what's possible. You can set expectations that guide your team toward a shared goal, ignite the spark of motivation when energy wanes, develop talent that creates future leaders, and cultivate collaboration that unites diverse perspectives into a symphony of success—all toward the goal of enabling performance.

Leading others is not easy, and just as superheroes face obstacles and challenges, you will encounter difficult moments—feedback that's hard to give, performance issues that seem insurmountable, or decisions that weigh heavily. But it's in these moments your leadership truly shines. Your superpower is your resilience, your ability to adapt, and your unwavering commitment to bringing out the best in others.

Ultimately, leadership is not about being the strongest or the fastest, but about empowering others to discover their strengths. It's about creating environments where people can thrive, achieve more than they imagined, and contribute in ways that bring your collective vision to life.

So, as you move forward, remember this: you have the tools, the knowledge, and the power to create a lasting impact. If you ever find yourself needing additional resources—whether it's templates, assessments, or just more guidance—visit my website at www.fullcircleconnections.ca or reach out via email at info@ sixfunctions.ca. These resources are here to support you in your leadership journey.

Now, it's time for you to lead, to inspire, and to drive performance that not only meets goals but unlocks potential in everyone around you.

Now use your superpower wisely and make this world a better place.

ACKNOWLEDGMENTS

I am deeply grateful to everyone who supported and believed in me during the creation of this book. Writing has been a journey of discovery and challenge, far more difficult than I ever imagined. Without the support, encouragement, feedback, and guidance of many people, this book would not exist.

To my family, especially my husband, Mark, and my sons, Tim and Tom, thank you for your unwavering love, patience, and belief in me—even when I was out of commission, completely absorbed in this project. And to my Mom, Czesia, thank you for teaching me perseverance. I would have quit if not for that.

To Carol and Joanne, you inspired me to do this work, and I am forever grateful for your teaching me, mentoring me, and helping me find a purpose and passion in my work.

Finally, to every participant in my training who was vulnerable, challenged me, offered kind words or advice, and told me I should write a book—thank you. Your openness and desire to grow helps me to learn, improve, and push forward.

ABOUT THE AUTHOR

DOROTHY KUDLA is a coach, workshop designer, keynote speaker, and the founder of Full Circle Connections, a training firm that helps organizations achieve objectives through strategic planning, leadership development, and individual contributor solutions. Dorothy has worked with global organizations across diverse industries, from Fortune 500 companies to emerging startups, specializing in aligning leadership, people, and culture to foster high performance and innovation.

Before launching her company, Dorothy led revenue operations at Hilton Hotels, where her passion for leadership development took root. Over the past two decades, she has built a reputation for developing practical and results-oriented programs that help leaders unlock the potential of their teams. Dorothy's approach is centered on empowering individuals to lead authentically, with a focus on trust, communication, and continuous growth.

A lifelong adventurer, Dorothy has completed several marathons and summited impressive peaks, including Mount Kilimanjaro, embodying a zest for life that mirrors her approach to leadership and personal growth. She is also an advocate for ongoing learning and transformation, believing that the best leaders are those who never stop growing themselves.

Dorothy holds multiple certifications in coaching and leadership, and has been recognized for her dynamic and engaging style, whether facilitating workshops or delivering keynote addresses. She lives in Toronto, Canada, with her husband, Mark, and their two sons, Tim and Tom.

www.ingramcontent.com/pod-product-compliance
Lightning Source LLC
Chambersburg PA
CBHW071331210326
41597CB00015B/1411